Published by
Periplus Editions (HK) Ltd.
with editorial offices at
153 Milk Street 5th Floor
Boston, MA 02109
Singapore 536983 and
5 Little Road #08-01
Singapore 536983

Printed in Singapore

ISBN: 962-593-592-4

ISBN: 962-593-923-7
(World ex Australia)

Publisher: Eric Oey
Cover Concept: Christina Ong
Production: Violet Wong

Photo Credits:
Food photographs by **Ashley Mackevicius.** All other photography by **John Hay**, except pages 12, 15 & 24, by **Esther Beaton**, Terra Australis Photo Agency, and pages 13, 28 & 30 by **Glenn Gibson,** Blitz Pictures.

Distributors

Asia Pacific
Berkeley Books Pte Ltd
5 Little Road #08-01
Singapore 536983
Tel: (65) 280-1330
Fax: (65) 280-6290

Indonesia
PT Java Books Indonesia
Jl. Kelapa Gading Kirana
Blok A14 No.17, Jakarta 14240
Tel: (62-21) 451-5351
Fax: (62-21) 453-4987

Japan
Tuttle Publishing
RK Building 2nd Floor
2-13-10 Shimo Meguro, Meguro-ku
Tokyo 153 0064
Tel: (81-3) 5437-0171
Fax: (81-3) 5437-0755

North America, Latin America and Europe
Tuttle Publishing
Distribution Center
Airport Industrial Park
364 Innovation Drive
North Clarendon, VT 05759-9436
Tel: (802) 773-8930, (800) 526-2778

Acknowledgements

The publisher gratefully acknowledges the enthusiastic support of Igal Bigos, Area Director, Food and Beverage Operations, of Hilton International Australia; his assistant, Jacqui Fink, and Rod Ritchie of Rainforest Publishing, who helped co-ordinate the project. The publisher also wishes to thank all those who lent props for photography, the contributing authors and, above all, the enthusiastic and talented chefs who so generously shared their culinary secrets.

THE FOOD OF AUSTRALIA

AUSTRALIA

Contemporary Recipes from Australia's Leading Chefs

Stephanie Alexander	Guido van Baelen
Maggie Beer	Beh Kim Un
Andrew Blake	Marieke Brugman
Cheong Liew	Gerda Eilts
Andrew Fielke	Bethany Finn
Herbert Franceschini	Paul Hoeps
Werner Kimmeringer	Alan Koh
Kurt Looser	Christine Manfield
Bill Marchetti	Paul Merrony
Damien Pignolet	Dietmar Sawyere
Alla Wolf-Tasker	Tetsuya Wakuda

Produced in association with Hilton International Australia
Food photography by Ashley Mackevicius
Styling by Wendy Berecry & Christina Ong
Edited by Wendy Hutton

PERIPLUS

Contents

Part One: Food in Australia

The new "cuisine of the southern sun"

by Tony Baker

Australia's contemporary cuisine has, over the past fifteen years or so, joined the ranks of the world's best, thanks to the dazzling range of local ingredients, a truly multicultural society and a new generation of boldly creative chefs. It is a perfect drawing together of flavours and styles: of French traditional and *nouvelle cuisine*, regional Italian and pan-Asian styles laced with cool Californian chic.

The evolution of the new cuisine seems to have taken place with startling swiftness. To write about Australian food a couple of decades ago would have been to invite disbelief, if not downright laughter, together with derisive remarks about kangaroo and emu steaks. While it is true that within a month of Captain Cook sighting his first kangaroo in 1770, a member of his party had eaten one, for most of the next two centuries, Australians aped the cooking styles of England, a country many still thought of as home, and one not particularly renowned for fine cuisine. It is also true that until the past decade, the wild fruits, vegetables, nuts and seeds used for some 40,000 years by the Aborigines were totally ignored by the more recent Australian arrivals.

With the huge influx of immigrants in the years following World War II, a largely Anglo-Celtic society was enriched, first by Europeans, then by Asians, as well as immigrants from countries as diverse as Chile and Iran. Today, Australian tastes are as cosmopolitan and multicultural as its population.

Australians, perhaps the best-travelled nation in the world, have experienced first hand the cuisines of Europe, Asia and America. So too have Australian chefs who, inspired by their experiences, have created a cuisine which benefits from the superb produce of this continental country, which produces everything from tropical fruits and herbs to cheese, wines and stunning seafood from the far south.

Australian cuisine emphasises freshness and shows great creativity in successfully blending cuisines from as far apart as Paris and Tokyo. This new "cuisine of the southern sun" complements the relaxed friendliness of modern Australia, and is as likely to be enjoyed on a verandah or in a courtyard as in a formal dining room.

Wine is integral to Australian dining, since this happiest of revolutions has gone hand in hand with the discovery, both at home and abroad, that the fresh, clean, flavour-packed wines of Australia are comparable with—if not better than—those of the old wine world.

As if all this were not enough, by the standards of other gourmet cuisines Australian food is remarkably cheap, as increasing numbers of tourists are discovering to their delight.

Page 2:
From the Indian Ocean on the west to the Pacific Ocean on the east, the Australian continent is a land of contrasts.
Opposite:
All the elements for a fine picnic on the beach: seafood, cheese, salad and wine.

An Endless Feast

A continent full of superb fresh produce

by Tony Baker

From diamonds and gold to oil, Australia is exceptionally well endowed with natural resources. But for food lovers the greatest blessing is a range of climates, ranging from alpine to tropical. Add rich, ancient soils, some of the purest waters on the planet and guaranteed sunshine and the result is an endless feast of produce.

Visit any big city market and this national feast will be temptingly arrayed before you. Visit the various states and territories and you will be offered particularly local ways of preparing the regional specialities, from the mangoes and mud crabs of Queensland to the apples and farmed salmon of Tasmania.

The cold waters of Tasmania, the island-state off the south of the Australian continent, are renowned for magnificent seafood, including succulent oysters.

Nowhere is this abundance more apparent than with Australian seafood, thanks to seas varying from warm to challengingly bracing, while the inland waterways contribute some unique crustaceans. To visit Queensland without tasting mud crabs and Moreton Bay bugs (similar to slipper or flathead lobsters) is to deprive yourself of two of life's intense pleasures. While you're there, you must also try such reef fish as red emperor, coral trout and pearl perch. In the Northern Territory as well as Queensland, barramundi fish, either large or small, is a must. Mention the Territory and you are reminded that Australian gourmets are increasingly partial to kangaroo, crocodile and buffalo. Traditional Territorians tuck into steaks that would embarrass folks in Argentina by their size. A popular local T-shirt has emblazoned on it the slogan "Eat beef, you bastards", a typically Australian approach to export promotion.

No visit to Sydney is complete without oysters and what Australians call "a feed of fish", such as John Dory or yellowfin tuna. Tasmania has a better than fair claim to being the seafood capital. The cool seas around this island state have long been prized for tasty deep-water fish such as trevally and blue grenadier, not to mention rock lobster, giant deep-sea crabs and scallops. Without doubt, though, Tasmania's gift to the world's gourmets has been the salmon produced in recent years from its fish farms, avidly sought whether fresh, smoked or sugar-cured. Move around Australia pausing only for plates of fish such as snapper and the King George whiting (a South Australian delicacy, entirely unlike the northern hemisphere whiting), or the magnificent abalone, yabbies (freshwater crayfish) and a cascade of prawns and you see why *sushi* bars have become so popular.

The same is true of fruit and nuts, as well as obvious joys such as mangoes, pineapples, pears and apples. The whole range of citrus—limes and mandarins and countless hectares of oranges—are arrayed across the southeast Australian heartland. Berry fruits, grapes eaten fresh or dried into raisins and sultanas, apricots and peaches likewise fresh or dried, giant watermelons and nuts such as Australia's own buttery, crunchy macadamias abound. Think of a fruit and you can be sure that if it does not already exist in commercial quantities, an enthusiast is pioneering its production somewhere between the Indian and Pacific oceans.

In southern Australia, olive groves and the pressings from wild olives now yield oils as distinctive as those of Italy and Spain. Mention of those two countries is an instant reminder that the contribution of immigrants, mainly European and Asian, to the national feast has not been confined to restaurants and market gardens. Australian

Nuts range from walnuts grown on farms like this one in Milawa, northern Victoria, to macadamias, originally known as Queensland bush nuts and indigenous to Australia.

other processed meats are of exceptional quality because the meat is good and because Italian, German, Polish and other producers brought ancient skills to their new homes. Italian pasta makers showed the way. Today's pasta makers are likely to be fifth generation Australians, and one must not forget the first generation Chinese noodle makers.

When it comes to meat, Australians take quality and quantity for granted. The Sunday roast leg of lamb would be an Australian food cliché were it not so gorgeously juicy and intensely flavoured, thanks to the lush well-watered pastures of southeast and southwestern Australia. Kangaroo meat has rapidly moved from pet food to an exotic delicacy to almost a staple. Close to a slightly gamey beef in taste, nutritionists like it for its low fat content. Emu meat

seems to be catching on the way kangaroo did; farmed venison is frequently found on menus and camel steaks have begun to make an appearance.

President Charles De Gaulle once said of his people: "The French will only be united under the threat of danger. Nobody can simply bring together a country that has 365 kinds of cheese." It won't be long before an Australian Prime Minister can make a similar remark.

Thanks to its sunshine and rainfall, Australia is perfect for dairying. Since the 1970s, when the missing element—the input of dedicated expert cheesemakers—was applied, the country began producing cheeses of international quality. Today, Australian gourmets avidly seek out the local products and cheese's share of the annual 500,000 tonnes of dairy exports is worth A$1 billion.

Southern Australia has led the charge in producing superb cheese, particularly the offshore islands of Tasmania, King Island in Bass Strait and Kangaroo Island off South Australia. On the mainland, the main cheese states are New South Wales, Victoria, South Australia and Western Australia. Although generic names such as cheddar, brie and camembert are rife, there is an increasing trend to coin names which reflect their origin, like the splendidly Australian True Blue, or embrace the place of origin, such as Mersey Valley and Milawa Blue.

Whatever your cheese preference, it is made in Australia. And yes, there is at least one cheese flavoured with gum leaves. Nor are Australia's cheeses confined to those from cow's and sheep's milk; there is a thriving goat's cheese industry making a range of products, including those hand-crafted

by Kervella in Western Australia.

From sugar to salt, if it crosses the taste buds, it will be made in Australia. I have spent some time trying to think of something essential to a first-class chef's output that Australia does not produce. The only product which came to mind is the truffle and, as you read this, some earnest prospector is doubtless hunting through loamy Australian undergrowth in the hope of striking it fungus rich.

A History of Australian Cuisine

From food gathering to an appreciation of fine food

by Michael Symons

"Is this all men can do with a new country? Look at those tin cans!" In his documentary novel, *Kangaroo*, D.H. Lawrence repeatedly describes Australia as rusty tin cans scattered over bare ground. In 1923, he found "towns—and corrugated iron—and millions of little fences—and empty tins".

When Europeans invaded the continent just over two centuries ago, Australia went from the highly integrated food gathering practised by the Aborigines to settled agriculture and grazing. This led to the sale of food in sacks and barrels, then bottles and cans, and finally to frozen and takeaway packs. Until recently, Australian food was the rapidly evolving cuisine of agribusiness, not a cuisine built on the love of fine food.

With the emergence of the grazing industry in the 19th century, bush workers were paid in rations called "Ten, Ten, Two & A Quarter" after the typical weekly issue of 10 lbs meat, 10 lbs flour, 2 lbs sugar and $\frac{1}{4}$ lb tea. In addition, the rations included salt and spirituous liquor. The meat, which had been salted pork or beef, became mutton slaughtered on the sheep station. Together, the rations provided a minimal diet which typically consisted of slabs of meat grilled on an open fire, heavy bread or "damper" baked in the ashes, overly sweetened tea boiled in a tin pot called a "billy", and drinks which were guzzled not for taste but intoxication.

The reformer Caroline Chisholm tried to civilise the place by conducting a public campaign to attract married couples and, especially, single women as immigrants. She distributed a booklet in London in 1847 entitled *Comfort for the Poor! Meat Three Times a Day!!* Promising meat at every meal was a compelling advertising slogan.

Remarking on the central culinary paradox of the country, a young French journalist, Edmond Marin La Meslée, wrote in 1883: "No other country on earth offers more of everything needed to make a good meal, or offers it more cheaply, than Australia: but there is no other country either where the cuisine is more elementary, not to say abominable."

Rough bush eating habits were civilised through improvements in the food industry. Prior to that, investments had been largely directed at primary production, and this generally meant wool. This made Australia little more than a basic "garden", and entrepreneurs had to turn their hands to the next step in the production chain—food processing and preparation. In the second half of the 19th century, the excitement shifted to food preservation and distribution. An Australian, James Harrison, has been credited with inventing mechanical refrigeration in 1851, and its first use was in long-distance shipping. Massive investment in railways opened up the hinterland to the growing of wheat, milk, sugar, fruit and vegetables.

From about the 1870s, factories turned out, among other products for both home and abroad, Rosella tomato sauce, Arnott's biscuits, IXL jams and MacRobertson's chocolates. Rollermills produced the white flour that became so symbolic of mass-produced food. While much of the country had been too hot for traditional brewing, in 1888 the Fosters brothers brought from the United States the technology for bottled lager beer, which relied on refrigeration, pasteurisation, bottom fermentation and bottling.

With this second great revolution (the industri-

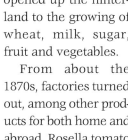

Schoolboys eating a typical lunch: a home-made Vegemite sandwich, a factory-made meat pie and a Chiko roll, a peculiarly local interpretation of the Chinese spring roll. Vegemite, a pungent spread made from yeast extract, is virtually an Australian icon.

alisation of food storage and distribution), Australian cooks advanced beyond the carcasses of meat, sacks of flour and chests of tea. They were encouraged to purchase packaged foods. In short, Australian households relied on those tin cans that caught the eye of D.H. Lawrence.

But from the 1890s, suburban housewives purchased local recipe books, even if they remained essentially re-arrangements of Eliza Acton's *Modern Cookery for Private Families of England*, written a half-century earlier. Each city adopted its culinary "bible", produced by the local gas company or a fund-raising group.

Australian women excelled at plain and decent cookery such as baked or roasted meats and vegetables. They also prided themselves on their puddings and cakes, relying on the iron kitchen range and the store cupboard's flour, sugar, cocoa, gelatine, desiccated coconut, and flavouring and colouring essences. Cooks swapped interesting recipes for sandwiches and cakes, and showed off skills at weekly "bring a plate" dances. Manufacturers issued recipe pamphlets which promoted their ingredients in "dainties" for polite morning and afternoon teas. The popular Lamington was cubes of cake coated in chocolate and coconut. The Pavlova—named after the ballerina Anna Pavlova and based on the New Zealand "meringue cake"— topped off the second stage in Australian cuisine, which was about to be transformed.

By the 1950s, food technologists had brought in the latest United States' know-how, which had been developed to feed Allied troops. This provided the technical, managerial and cultural foundation for the vertically-integrated and generally foreign-owned agribusiness. At the same time, the wartime steelworks and munitions factories had been turned over to producing motor vehicles and refrigerators.

We need to appreciate the key role of private cars and refrigerators in the development of the supermarket. Until the 1950s, carters delivered much household food daily from door-to-door, or the housewives took their string-bags to the corner store. Now, the car enabled the family to collect the shopping weekly from the more distant supermarket. Once home, milk and meat were now kept in the fridge.

The food industry's goal was not only to grow and preserve food in sophisticated ways, but now also to cook it. The archetypal "convenience" dish, the TV Dinner, was to be a complete meal frozen in a re-heatable aluminium tray, although it was less successful than a range of dried Chinese meals, frozen pizzas, pre-mixed cakes and Coca-Cola.

Restaurants and cafés grew in number and Australian families who had never dined out now took to well-priced and well-prepared Chinese meals; opinion-leaders hobnobbed in fashionable bistros. Since the 1960s, cookery books have also proliferated and diversified.

This arrival of global cuisine has usually been attributed to Australia's strong post-war immigration programme. Certainly, Australian society is now markedly multicultural. However, it had previously been a "mixing-pot" without accepting Italian, Chinese or other cooking. The latest culinary development is the "discovery" of Australia's indigenous ingredients.

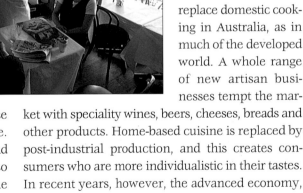

Eating out in restaurants and cafés is now very much part of the modern Australian lifestyle.

Today, convenience products, fast food and restaurants threaten to replace domestic cooking in Australia, as in much of the developed world. A whole range of new artisan businesses tempt the market with speciality wines, beers, cheeses, breads and other products. Home-based cuisine is replaced by post-industrial production, and this creates consumers who are more individualistic in their tastes. In recent years, however, the advanced economy, technical expertise and "foodie" enthusiasms have put Australians at the forefront of global cooking. Now not just from cans, well-informed eaters enjoy the full fruits of the earth.

Native Australian Food

The rediscovery of ancient indigenous ingredients

by Andrew Fielke

Australia's newest cuisine paradoxically depends upon its oldest ingredients. When white settlers first arrived in Australia a little over two centuries ago, the country's Aborigines—who had inhabited the continent for some 40,000 years—had a remarkable understanding of its natural resources. However, it is in only in the last decade or so that the non-Aboriginal population of Australia has begun to discover its exciting range of indigenous food, not only obvious items such as kangaroo meat but a variety of wild seeds, nuts, fruit and vegetables known to the natives for thousands of years. Ironically, much of this ancient knowledge was in danger of being lost as many Aborigines left their traditional homelands and adopted new lifestyles.

The Aborigines' spiritual bonding with their land and their knowledge of its produce had been handed down from one generation to the next by their legends and stories. The first white settlers in Australia, noting that the natives were not agriculturalists in the accepted sense, dismissed them as simple hunters and gatherers. It has since been discovered that the Aborigines irrigated some areas of land, regulated the undergrowth and encouraged regrowth and genetic diversity by practising controlled burning of the vegetation. Certain abundant food resources were actively managed and maintained. Seeds of fruits were often scattered after eating, and when eggs of the magpie goose were taken, a few nests were always left untouched. In South Australia, the Aborigines stored excess live fish from their catch in special traps.

Most foods were eaten raw, but some required special treatment such as roasting or pounding and leaching in running water to remove harmful toxins. Some foodstuffs were cooked, with witchetty grubs, kangaroos, smaller mammals, crabs, birds and fish being roasting over a fire. Wattle and Kurrajong seeds were roasted on red-hot coals, ground to a flour, mixed with water and baked to make a nutritious damper or seed cake.

The recent discovery of indigenous ingredients

Aboriginal rock paintings in the Northern Territory show an emu and a lizard, both of which would have been roasted over a fire before being eaten.

by non-Aboriginal Australians was made possible largely by Vic Cherikoff, a research scientist at Sydney University, who was the first person to commence commercial collection and distribution of a range of native foods through his then fledgling company, Bush Tucker Supply Australia, in 1987. His company, and others like South Australia's Creative Native Australian Industries, distribute a wide range of native ingredients. From the handful of Australian chefs who initially took up the challenge of incorporating Australian native foods into modern and conventional recipes, there is now an ever-increasing acceptance of, and interest in, such ingredients.

A dragon lizard ready for the fire. A wide variety of seeds were also roasted on red-hot coals before being ground to make a nutritious flour.

The range of fruits, herbs, spices and nuts available has increased considerably, with responsible companies ensuring the sustainability of such wild foods through the practice of ecologically sound farming. Such companies also grow and market Australian native food plants for sale to commercial produce growers and home gardeners, and some also manufacture a range of gourmet food products made from the plants and fauna species. At the same time, there has been a proliferation of emu, yabby and barramundi farms.

Today's Australians have the unique good fortune to be able to use fruits, nuts, seeds, herbs, tubers, vegetables and animals just as they were some 40,000 years ago, unmanipulated by man through genetic engineering or selective breeding.

Restaurants like Adelaide's Red Ochre Grill are helping introduce Australia's age-old bush foods to a wider audience, and the consistent success and international attention over the years demonstrates that the concept of a creative indigenous cuisine is far more than just a fad. Native foods are slowly but surely being integrated into Australian cuisine, although it is unlikely that large numbers of Australian restaurants will become dedicated "bush food" restaurants. Young Australian chefs now have the opportunity to use Australia's oldest ingredients to develop a fresh and innovative style of cuisine limited only by their imagination.

Mediterranean Influences

Australia moves from damper to focaccia

by Tess Mallos

O ne often-quoted statistic which reveals just how many immigrants from the Mediterranean have made Australia their home is that Melbourne has the third biggest population of people of Greek origin anywhere in the world, including Greece.

The immigration of hundreds of thousands of Mediterraneans—primarily Italians, Greeks and Lebanese—has had a profound impact on the cuisine of Australia, yet the changes in mainstream eating patterns happened only relatively recently.

As far back as the 1880s, small numbers of immigrants from Italy, Greece, Cyprus, Lebanon, Syria, Malta and Spain began arriving. In 1947, acknowledging the country's severe manpower shortage, the government decided that more immigrants were needed if Australia was to reach its full potential. By this time, only 2% of the population of 7.5 million was of non-Anglo-Celtic origin and the government continued targeting the British so that Australia's Anglo culture could be maintained.

But it was necessary to also include continental Europeans if Australia's population was to grow quickly. Displaced persons of Northern Europe and other Europeans were allowed, with large intakes from Latvia, Estonia, Lithuania, Poland, Holland, Germany, Austria, Czechoslovakia, Hungary, Romania, Yugoslavia, Italy, Greece and Malta. By 1991, almost 18 percent of the population—which had more than doubled to 16.5 million since 1947—did not speak English in the home. Today, Italians are the largest immigrant group after those from the UK and Ireland.

While Australia could provide the basic ingredients to allow these "New Australians" to maintain their dietary preferences, they were initially obliged to turn to their own gardens and to their own expertise in the kitchen. They made their own breads, yoghurt, some cheeses, preserved meats and pasta, supplementing these with special foods imported by a few Italian, Greek and Lebanese stores.

Back in the 1940s, our "Greek" country garden provided us with the many vegetables and herbs not

A group of Italian Australians in Perth, Western Australia; Italians form the country's largest immigrant group after settlers from the United Kingdom and Ireland.

eaten by Australians of Anglo-Celtic background, as did the gardens of immigrant Italians and Lebanese. A number of Italians then set up market gardens to supply the many Italian-owned fruit and vegetable shops catering to the needs of the general public, as well as customers of Mediterranean background.

Because of the rapid increase in the numbers of immigrants arriving from the 1950s onwards, there was a greater opportunity to manufacture the foods they sought on a commercial scale, such as salamis, prosciutto, pepperoni and other preserved meats, Italian and Greek cheeses, yoghurt, pasta and filo pasty. The ready availability of such products now made it possible for other Australians to become familiar with hitherto exotic foodstuffs.

Today, pizza and pasta are very much part of the Australian diet, as are Lebanese/Syrian tabouli and hommus, Greek tzatziki and taramosalata. There are olives galore, and sun-dried tomatoes became so popular in the mid 1980s that imports are now competing with Australian-made products, along with sun-dried capsicums. Italian and Greek breads (including the immensely popular focaccia) are now readily available—a vast change from the colonial bush bread or damper—and Lebanese pocket or pita breads are also firmly entrenched.

The majority of Australians in the past had an aversion to oil of any kind and the oiliness of Greek and Italian food was often criticised. The acceptance of olive oil began only when National Heart Foundation began urging Australians in the 1970s to replace some of their traditional butter, lard and dripping with poly-unsaturated oils. Recent research has indicated that the incidence of heart dis-

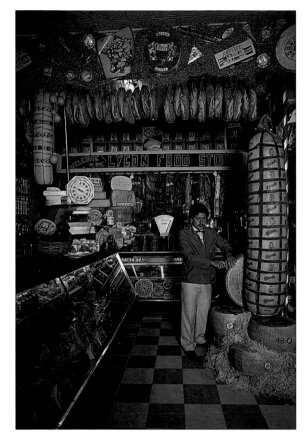

The large influx of immigrants from Mediterranean countries after WWII provided the impetus for the manufacture of a wide range of cheeses, processed meats, pasta and other products. This typical delicatessen is in Melbourne's Lygon Street.

ease is lower among those following a "Mediterranean diet", with a high intake of complex carbohydrates (pasta, rice, bread and burghul), vegetables and fruits, with more seafood than meat, plenty of pulses and olive oil, a mono-saturated oil.

Australians in the 1990s are the largest per capita consumers of olive oil outside the Mediterranean countries. This is a far cry from the 1940s, when the only olive oil in easy reach was in tiny bottles at the

That old British stalwart, roast lamb, is more likely to be enhanced with garlic and rosemary these days, thanks to the influence of Mediterranean cuisines.

In the early years of their culinary awakening, the first taste many Australians had of Mediterranean foods was during their "continental tours", when they had no option but to try salamis, pizzas, olives, strong cheeses, pasta or moussaka. Back home, with taste buds primed, they were more willing to accept the new foods gradually appearing in the market place. Food columnists were also responsible in the process of education, and when Australian-produced cookbooks began specialising in the cuisines of various countries because the basic foods were finally readily available and had gained acceptance, Australians could experiment with alacrity.

Finally, restaurants have always played a part. Australia was not a total culinary wilderness in the early days. There were Italian restaurants in Melbourne from the early 1920s, and in other areas there were many other restaurants featuring cuisines described as "Continental" and "French". These days, Italian restaurants abound, together with Greek and Lebanese/Syrian restaurants, while Spanish restaurants are increasing in popularity. Many restaurateurs, recognising the suitability of Mediterranean food to Australia's climate and lifestyle, take the best of these foods which Australia now produces, combining them with skill and imagination and presenting their bill of fare as "Mediterranean-style".

pharmacy, its use confined to medicinal remedies and baby care.

Natural or "health food" stores catering principally to vegetarians were another factor in popularising Mediterranean foods. Bulgur, the steamed crushed wheat of the Eastern Mediterranean, first became available to the general public through such outlets, as did yoghurt, tahini, pulses and, more recently, the couscous of Morocco.

The embarrassments of my youth—admitting to using olive oil on salads and vegetables, and eating "soured" milk (yoghurt)—are unknown to my children and grandchildren; they can and do enjoy openly whatever they like in our culinarily enlightened society.

Australia's Asian Connection

Asian immigration has had a dramatic culinary impact

by Charmaine Solomon

From a culinary point of view, Australia is not the same country we migrated to 36 years ago, when we left the tropical island of Ceylon (now Sri Lanka) for Sydney—big, beautiful, bewildering. Forward scouts had warned us that Australia was a land where one could buy nothing in the way of "civilised" foods and that we should take our own supplies of spices.

Heeding the advice, I came armed with tins of curry powder my mother had blended for me. On the tin was written, in her clear script, a basic recipe. With this as my lifeline, I was launched on the unknown waters of cooking real food for the first time. ("Real food" meaning meals to survive on, as distinct from the cakes and confectionery I had taken pleasure in creating.) There had been no need for me to prepare meals in Sri Lanka because every household had a resident cook. While there was a "sink or swim" feeling of being thrown in at the deep end, there was also a sense of real adventure.

This was the time of the White Australia policy. In order to obtain permission to settle in Australia, I had to provide proof of the requisite 75 percent of European blood. (Thankfully, my ancestors had arrived in Ceylon from Holland in the year 1714 and detailed genealogies of many Dutch families had been kept by the Dutch Burgher Union.) The cultural cringe was alive and well in Australia, but it was the newcomers who suffered from it. I learned to make spaghetti Bolognese and roasts almost before I learned to make a good curry.

When it came to grocery shopping, apart from the corner store with its basic supplies, there existed only the "Ham and Beef" shop, forerunner of today's delicatessen, but at that time the name was totally descriptive. There were also health food stores where one could purchase rice, split peas, curry powder and turmeric.

But what a difference the last three decades have made in the eating habits of Australians of Anglo-Celtic background, to whom the "baked dinner" was almost a religion, with services being held at least once a week; to whom a curry was what you did with the leftover roast and Chinese food the invention known as *chop suey*.

Now Australians delight in the opportunity of travelling through their taste buds, and often the journey takes them to Asia. *Yum cha* (*dim sum*) on weekends is becoming increasingly popular. If a Thai restaurant is known to be good, you had better book reservations. Indian restaurants are gaining popularity, especially those that offer regional or vegetarian food. Eat-in or take-away places specialise in noodles from Malaysia, *pho* from Vietnam, *laksa* from Singapore, satay and other quick meals.

It's hard to believe that a generation ago, the average Aussie considered it the height of chic to visit the local Chinese restaurant. The sign outside assured the clientele that "Chinese and Australian" meals were served, and the menu was carefully vetted so that nothing too challenging confronted customers.

I think the change may have started with tourism to Asia. With their country placed in the Pacific, nearer to Asia than to Europe or America, holidays in Asia are more affordable to average Australians. Once travellers were exposed to the excellent, bargain-priced food, there was no going back. They came home to Australia keen to repeat their gastronomic experiences, even if it meant learning to cook the food themselves. They'd seen it tossed together in minutes at street stalls and felt it couldn't be too difficult—and it isn't.

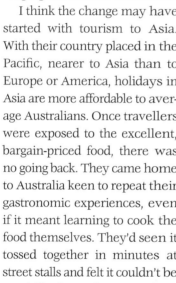

In the 1960s, the emphasis was on Continental cuisines with their richness and long cooking methods. It has now shifted to Asian cuisines with fresh flavours and the fast, healthy cooking styles of steaming and stir-frying. I am fortunate to have lived in Australia during decades of incredible change and had the opportunity to share my love of Asian cooking through books and teaching. When referred to as the "mother of Asian cooking in Australia", I protest that I was only a midwife, merely easing its entry into this new area and sharing with others what I had to learn myself, how to cook Asian food in a Western country. I had a hard time convincing people that all Asian food did not have to be loaded with chilli. I learned not to wince when some earnest cook assured me that she made a "curry" with diced apples, bananas, sultanas and curry powder.

Chinese food was everything in a sweet and sour sauce, or deep fried (including the ice-cream); Indonesian food was hot *sambals* which made tears run; Indian food was *pappadams* and cucumbers in yoghurt and curries with no depth of flavour, no subtle fragrant spices but lots of chilli powder. If not hot they were considered not "authentic", so one might say the public got what they deserved. As for Thai, Vietnamese, Cambodian, Laotian, Japanese, Nonya, Burmese, Korean cuisines—the palette of flavours now enrapturing many Australians—they were not even blips on the horizon.

In the 1960s, I used to write to my family in Sri Lanka for stocks of spices. In the 1970s, Asian ingredients started to become more accessible, mainly in the Chinatown areas of capital cities. In the 1980s, because of the influx of Asian immigrants and refugees, there was a quantum leap in growing and distributing numerous Asian herbs, vegetables and fruits. Chilli sauces and other flavourings began to be produced locally. Now, in this country with its Western heritage, one is able to purchase almost as wide a range of Asian ingredients as in Asia itself.

Looking back over 25 years of food writing, I can see from my early books that at first there was no choice but to use dried curry leaves, lemon grass and galangal, and explain to readers how to make coconut milk since a quality product was not available in cans. Now, while some remote country towns might still be reliant on dried herbs, it is most unlikely that the supermarket does not carry at least a couple of brands of canned coconut milk.

In the big cities, every suburban shopping centre has an Asian supermarket, perhaps more than one. The aisles buzz with activity, especially at weekends. The customers are not all Asian either. Young chefs who are not afraid of blazing trails are making a mockery of the well known lines penned by Rudyard Kipling, "East is East and West is West and never the twain shall meet." In the capable hands of today's high-profile chefs, ingredients and cooking methods of both East and West are meeting and merging. The result is an exciting blend in which neither one predominates, but each enhances the other.

Australia is emerging from the shadow of "the old country", finding its place in the Asia-Pacific region and realising that the cuisines of its Asian neighbours are more relevant to its climate than those of Europe. The great land extending from the tropics to the south allows Australians to enjoy the gamut from mangoes, rambutans, kaffir limes, pandan leaves, crabs of dinner-plate size, to Atlantic salmon and ocean trout from the icy waters off Tasmania.

Asian vegetables are now eagerly sought by Australians of all ethnic backgrounds.

There is an exploration taking place, a happy discovery of new ingredients and fresh flavours. East and West are not only meeting, they are embracing. The coating of chopped *konbu* (sea kelp) on the rare slice of ocean trout, the Indian *tandoori* marinade on a char-grilled kangaroo fillet, the snow peas and fresh water chestnut in the salad, the threads of Thai lime leaf and slivers of lemon grass in a tomato broth, the hint of galangal in the crab-filled ravioli perhaps give us proof of an emerging uniquely Australian cuisine.

MacDonnell Ranges outside Alice Springs, where restaurateur Ron Tremaine provides billy tea, damper, bush salad and Territory beef served under the stars—an experience not to be forgotten. I think the original Australian joke is the bushman's recipe for cooking cockatoo. Catch a cockatoo and boil it with two stones. When the stones are soft, the bird is ready. Another version commands you to throw away the cockatoo and eat the stones. Another bush recipe calls for 3 medium-size camels, 700 bushels of vegetables, 1,000 gallons of gravy and 2 small rabbits. You are directed to spend several months preparing and simmering the stew, which will serve 3,800; if more people are expected, add the 2 rabbits.

The final touch to any Aussie barbecue is a handful of gum leaves in the fire for that dinky di (authentic) out-back flavour.

Thanks to its climate, eating out around Australia is also a mass affair. Rare is the Australian event, from the running of the Melbourne Cup to the Adelaide arts festival, which does not feature outdoor eating, usually around a "barbie", perhaps a picnic or that sturdy Australian staple, meat pie with tomato sauce.

When Victoria embarked on a tourism promotion campaign, the promoters did so with the world's longest lunch at which hundreds of people sat down to seafood on a long pier. There are now at least a dozen regional wine and food festivals in which premier restaurants set up in wine cellar doors for a day or weekend and people travel the district for a glass of wine and plate of food at each.

Despite the national passion for the outdoors, it is only in recent years that what seems the most obvious way of enjoying this has caught on. Australia's liquor licensing laws and local council regulations once made pavement or boulevard eating and drinking impossible. Battle was joined and won and today, entire city streets from Fremantle in Western Australia to the tourist belts of Queensland are now lined with tables and chairs. That alfresco feeling is also an integral part of many frontline restaurants. Where once the backyard was the place for the empties, today it is likely to be a shaded garden with foodies taking their ease. When making a booking at an Australian restaurant, it's wise to check the weather forecast and then inquire whether there is an outdoor option.

The national partiality for eating outdoors has perhaps also contributed to Australians' longevity. From bush tucker to barbies, Australians have learnt the simple pleasures of the plain grill and taught themselves to be inventive when devising salads. Paul Hogan's shrimp on the barbie was a health as well as a lifestyle statement.

Gourmet Dining in the Country

The transformation of the Australian countryside

by Marieke Brugman

Only a generation ago, the prospect of a handsome dining room, a fine meal and superb wines away from an Australian metropolis would have been merely fanciful, unless one had the good fortune to be visiting a traditional farming family. In less than twenty years, there has been a virtual revolution across the countryside, both in terms of the variety of choices of character-rich places to stay overnight and to eat regionally focused cuisine, and in terms of the agricultural landscape itself.

Long anchored in largely Anglo-Celtic traditions, the rural landscape was dominated by sheep, cattle and wheat. The farms (known as stations) supported the extended families of the rural "gentry" as well as their workers and families, and because of their isolation, were virtually self-sufficient.

The enclave of buildings would have included a schoolhouse, stables, shearing sheds, outlying buildings for machinery and repairs, and a meathouse in which to hang home-killed carcasses. Meat, because of its bountifulness, tended to form the major dietary staple. Rabbit and wild duck in season were shot for the table, poultry raised, the house cow milked, an orchard kept and a vegetable garden tended. Bulk dry-foods would be procured on long, infrequent forays to the nearest "town".

Homestead kitchens were the norm and the hub of social life. Huge wood-burning stoves allowed the preparation of copious quantities of food. A secondary kitchen or separate space was devoted to the processing and preserving of jams, pickles, chutneys and sauces. Often there was a stone-lined cellar beneath for the storage of orderly rows of preserving jars with their aesthetic placements of fruit and vegetables. Roast dinners were typical of fare which could be characterised as plain, simple, hearty, honest cooking with "fancy" cooking reserved for the dessert repertoire.

Much of this is now a thing of the past, yet never before have the gastronomic opportunities in country Australia been more bright. The increasingly adventurous and curious nature of the Australian

One of the many hundreds of delicious options throughout the Australian countryside, the Uraidla Aristologist in the Adelaide hills offers excellent cuisine.

Country-fresh produce can be enjoyed in restaurants, cafés, country homes or simply on a picnic.

variations on steak and chips or a mixed grill), Victoria's spectacularly scenic Great Ocean Road is now known as "the cappuccino coast", testament to a myriad of cafés serving proper coffee, lovely wines, and everything from focaccia and pasta to fresh salads and local grilled fish.

Along with dynamic changes in agriculture—partly the result of leading chefs encouraging producers and growers to diversify—so too the countryside is reinventing itself. One of the earliest examples of a new rural identity was the pioneering Howqua Dale Gourmet Retreat, founded in 1977 in the glorious sub-alpine region of north-eastern Victoria. Howqua Dale was one of the first properties in Australia to take advantage of its beautiful location and to offer city guests a unique combination of an authentic bush environment with a highly refined sense of Australian hospitality, luxurious accommodation, soothing views and superb food with excellent wines from a mostly Australian cellar. The cuisine is proudly Australian and draws for its inspiration on what is locally available during the season: herbs and vegetables from the garden, wild mushrooms gathered from nearby fields and forests,

palate has not confined itself to city sophistication. From the 1950s, when Australians started to enjoy a somewhat Westernised rendition of Chinese food, they have consistently expanded their repertoire of flavours, so that now even ordinary households all over the country include ginger, garlic, fresh coriander and basil in their weekly shopping lists.

Where once the dining options outside major cities were limited to a counter-meal at a pub (basic chestnuts, walnuts, honey and berries from neighbouring farms, wine from the next valley at Delatite, venison and salmon from the Yarra Valley and eggs from free-roving "chooks".

There are now hundreds of opportunities for city residents and overseas visitors to explore an intricate tapestry of establishments flung far and wide, which are testament to Australia as a paradise for food and wine lovers.

One of the newest but most remote properties, Haggerstone Island in Far North Queensland, gives a unique experience to the tiny number of visitors it takes at any one time. Totally self-sufficient in its tropical environment where an abundance of fish virtually jump out of the water, each day's meals rely entirely on what has been picked, netted, speared or caught that day. Coral trout, sardines, coconuts, exotic fruits and hot-climate vegetables, so extraordinarily fresh they need little adornment, remind urbanites of the rare experience of enjoying the wonderful flavours and texture of ingredients which are still "alive". And the holiday is much enhanced for guests because they participate in the daily harvest and preparation of communal meals.

It is doubtful that Australia has or will develop distinctively regional cuisines, partly because chefs are spoiled by their easy access to such a huge variety of ingredients. However, chefs such as Maggie Beer (whose Pheasant Farm in South Australia gave a new meaning to regional food) demonstrated the value of cooking so close to the source. She was responsible for creating significant dishes which celebrated a region's specialities, and also subtly commented on their particular rural culture and the importance of "natural" and unadulterated food.

These attitudes continue to exert a widespread influence over the practices of country cooks. Kate Lamont, one of the rising young stars in Western Australia, has created a cuisine at her family's winery in the Swan Valley that is based on those ingredients most readily available to her. These include outstanding goat cheese made by one of Australia's leading cheese makers, Gay Kervella, who runs her organically managed farm on a remote and beautiful peak in the next valley surrounded by national park; marron (freshwater crayfish) farmed in ponds up the road; olive oil and sour dough bread produced at an old monastery in New Norcia; and vegetables and fruit from neighbours.

Many of Australia's wine regions have become the hub for a new form of country culture. A number of wineries have created their own restaurants and cooks are establishing their businesses in wine-growing locales, with the emphasis on country fresh foods and highlighting of regional wines. From grand and luxurious to simple, rustic old homesteads, elaborately decorated country pubs, wonderful manor houses and picturesque stone cottages have been brought back to life. Redolent of a bygone era and encapsulating the spirit of a region, they offer modern comfort in individualistic settings.

The Australian countryside is becoming a haven for food cognoscenti, especially for travellers curious to experience a way of life which harks back to some old-fashioned values in terms of friendship and generosity, but which is also touched by the modern influences of the multi-ethnic, eclectic society which makes Australian cities exciting.

Part Two: Chefs, Ingredients & Recipes
The Chefs of Australia
by Rita Erlich

What exactly is Australian cooking? It's open-minded, it's skilled, it's not weighted down by tradition and, as a profession, it attracts some of the best minds in the country. Australia is where some of the finest chefs have had no formal culinary training, and where the proportion of great women cooks is much higher than anywhere else.

There are in fact two aspects of Australian food. The first is the ingredients, all those distinctively Australian items such as kangaroo and emu and bush tomatoes and bunya nuts. But there's also Australian food in terms of how ingredients are cooked and served by Australians. It is this second aspect of food that makes eating in Australia so rewarding, and as the following recipes show, it is the striking amalgam of styles and ingredients that distinguishes Australian cooks.

You can never be sure what you'll eat next. It might be a savoury pumpkin risotto cake with smoked kangaroo as Bethany Finn of the Adelaide Hilton makes it. It might be a chicken breast on couscous mixed with pomegranate seeds and served with pistachio butter as prepared by Andrew Blake. It could be a mousse of snapper and prawns wrapped in a *nori* omelette created by Christine Manfield. It might be Marieke Brugman's classic pavlova, a meringue dessert regarded as an Australian classic, or a cheesecake made from native Illawarra plums as prepared by Guido van Baelen of the Sydney Airport Hilton.

Most modern cooking, whatever the country, now has an international flavour. To some extent, fine cooking has always been international, and it has been the strength of the Hilton hotel chain that it provided fine dining restaurants where the quality of cooking and excellence of service were hallmarks. In the late 60s and 70s, when grand restaurants were few, the Hilton dining rooms were standard bearers and important training grounds for cooks and waiters.

The formality and hierarchy of international hotel kitchens is often different from the easier structure of Australian restaurant kitchens, but there is a fruitful exchange of dialogue between the two styles. The Hilton now often showcases Australian chefs in the way that French chefs used to appear for limited seasons. The Melbourne Hilton, for example, invited three top Australian chefs (including Paul Merrony and Cheong Liew, who have contributed to this book) to limited seasons in the prestigious Cliveden Room Restaurant. Herbert Franceschini at the Brisbane Hilton launched an ongoing guest chef programme which has honoured Australian chefs.

Opposite:
Typical of the new breed of innovative young chefs, Andrew Blake is always on the move.

Australia's top chefs have played their part in encouraging growers and suppliers. Australia has a remarkably fine range of produce and a growing number of specialised producers who are able to continue and even flourish because of a network of enterprising and dedicated chefs. One chef might find a specialist producing corn-fed chickens or exquisite baby beans, or a supplier of Illawarra plums or bush tomatoes, but everyone will soon know about them. It is not unknown for chefs to telephone one another for information: "Where did you get your squab?" "What's your source for warrigal greens?" Stephanie Alexander is particularly good at tracking down ingredients and suppliers, and her book, *Stephanie's Australia*, is a comprehensive guide to the best Australian food and its producers.

There's a new kind of internationalism in cooking now. The United States has been particularly innovative with a range of mixed cuisines. English-speaking countries, Australia included, are going through an East-meets-West phase, as indeed are many Asian countries. One reason for the international flavours is that chefs and restaurateurs travel. They all see the same new books and magazines and study the same photographs. What is hot in New York one week will soon appear on tables in London, Melbourne and Sydney.

But Australia's food internationalism is slightly different. Australia is an immigrant country, with each successive wave of immigration bringing its own food and flavours. Consider the origins of many of the chefs who have contributed to this book. Cheong Liew came from Malaysia, Marieke Brugman's parents were born in Holland, Alla Wolf-Tasker was born in Vienna of Russian parents, Dietmar Sawyere's father was Swiss, Beh Kim Un is Malaysian-born, Bill Marchetti's parents were Italian and German, Tetsuya Wakuda is Japanese.

What makes the immigrant tradition so special is that all those disparate backgrounds and cooking traditions have blended into a multicultural mainstream. Consider what the Australian-born chefs do: Christine Manfield offers a tea-smoked yellowfin tuna with a sweet and sour fennel salad; Stephanie Alexander uses Moroccan-inspired preserved lemon with Tasmanian salmon; Bethany Finn seasons roast lamb with Middle-Eastern *harissa* and accompanies it by Indian chick pea curry and *naan* bread. In the kitchen, everyone is multilingual.

A surprising proportion of Australia's top chefs began their careers in other fields. They are not chefs in the European tradition, people who trained in the industry from a tender age. Their experiences before turning to restaurants inform their views of food and cooking, and are perhaps responsible for their open-minded approach.

Their recipes keep developing. For example, Paul Merrony's salad of turnips and roast tomatoes began as a simple salad of roast tomatoes, a minimalist dish that was a revelation at a time when the number of ingredients and garnishes on the plate was meant to be an index of quality. It has been modified over the years, another point of difference with European chefs whose dishes may remain unchanged for twenty years.

The recipes in this book represent a cross-section of the best Australian contemporary cuisine. In short, these are the tastes of Australia.

Australian Ingredients

*Australian cuisine draws on ingredients
from around the world*

BASIL, THAI: The most commonly used Thai basil in Australia is *horapa*; it has a distinct fragrance but European sweet basil can be substituted.

BLACK MUSTARD SEEDS: Used in Indian-influenced dishes; do not substitute with yellow mustard seeds.

BLACK ONION SEEDS: Sometimes known as nigella, these seeds (called *kalonji* in India) should be available in Indian stores; black sesame seeds could be substituted.

BUNYA NUTS: Starchy nuts from the cone of the bunya pine native to Australia. They are similar in taste and texture to chestnuts, although each bunya nut contains about five times as much meat as a chestnut.

BUSH TOMATOES: Sometimes known as desert raisins, these small intensely-flavoured berries grow on a native shrub related to the tomato. Substitute with sun-dried tomatoes.

CHILLIES: The most commonly used chillies are finger-length red or green fresh chillies and the tiny, much hotter bird's-eye chillies.

CLOUD EAR FUNGUS: Also known as wood fungus, this is a shrivelled greyish-brown fungus which swells to at least four times its original size after soaked in warm water for 10–15 minutes.

CORIANDER LEAF: Fresh coriander leaves, known in some countries as cilantro, are popular in many dishes with a Southeast Asian inspiration. The roots are also used in Thai

Basil

Native Australian products can be purchased in a number of speciality shops in major Australian cities and can also be ordered directly from:

Australian Native Produce Industries
P.O. Box 163
Paringa
South Australia 5340
Australia

Bunya Nuts

Bush Tucker Supply Australia
P.O. Box B103
Boronia Park
New South Wales 2111
Australia

Bush Tomatoes

Illawarra Plums

Kaffir Lime Leaf

Lemon Aspen

Lemon Myrtle Leaves

cuisine. Any Asian store or market and many regular Australian supermarkets and vegetable shops sell fresh coriander leaf.

COUSCOUS: Semolina grains popular in Middle Eastern cooking, sold in packets and generally pre-cooked.

CRÈME FRAÎCHE: A slightly soured thick cream used in French cooking; look for it in supermarkets or combine thick cream with a little plain yoghurt.

FISH SAUCE: A pungent salty sauce used in Thai and Vietnamese cuisine.

GALANGAL: A rhizome which is a member of the ginger family, galangal is widely used in Southeast Asian cuisine and should be available fresh in any Asian market. Alternatively, jars of water-packed galangal exported from Thailand can be used as a substitute.

HIJIKI: Japanese seaweed, generally available dried; soak in warm water until swollen.

ILLAWARRA PLUMS: Dark red berries from the native Brown Pine, these have a rich berry flavour and can be substituted with any small purple or red plums.

JAPANESE HORSERADISH: Widely referred to by its Japanese name, *wasabi*, this comes from a root that is not a true horseradish, although it shares the same nose-tingling properties. Although sold ready-mixed in tubes, it is preferable to buy tins of *wasabi* powder and mix to a paste with water shortly before using.

KAFFIR LIME LEAF: The intensely fragrant leaf of the kaffir or leprous lime tree is used in Southeast Asian, particularly Thai, dishes. Available fresh in speciality shops.

LAVER: A seaweed widely used in Japanese cuisine and known as *nori*, this is sold in packets and is normally toasted and crisp. If it has gone soggy, hold over a flame for a few seconds to regain its crispness. *Nori* is also sold seasoned and eaten as a snack.

LEMON ASPEN: These small pale lemon-coloured fruits which are native to the tropical regions of Australia have a sharp citrus flavour. Use lemon juice as a substitute.

LEMON GRASS: A lemon-scented grass found throughout Southeast Asia and now grown in warmer areas of Australia, this looks like a miniature leek. Use only the bottom 10 cm (4 in) of the stalk. Available in most Asian stores and markets.

LEMON MYRTLE LEAVES: Similar in fragrance to lemon verbena, these come from a native rainforest tree; kaffir lime leaves make a good substitute.

MACADAMIA NUT: An Australian native also known as the Queensland bush nut, this was popularised by American growers in Hawaii.

MARRON: A fresh-water crayfish native to

Australia, this expensive delicacy is now being pond-reared. Any other crustacean such as yabby (see below), flathead lobster or slipper lobster (known in Australia as Moreton Bay or Balmain bugs) can be used as a substitute.

MIRIN: A sweet Japanese rice wine used only in cooking. Keeps indefinitely.

MORETON BAY BUGS: This is the Queensland term for the slipper or flathead lobster, *Thenus orientalis,* found throughout the Indo-Pacific region.

PALM SUGAR: Used in Southeast Asian cooking, this is made from the sap of the inflorescences of the aren or coconut palm. If not available, substitute soft brown sugar with a touch of maple syrup.

POLENTA: A fine cornmeal popular in Italy, this is usually boiled and allowed to cool into firm cakes, which are then fried or grilled. Sold in packets in any speciality store and many supermarkets.

SAKE: Japanese rice wine, which keeps up to one month after opening; if unavailable, substitute with Chinese rice wine for cooking.

SHALLOT: Small clusters of what look like miniature onions with brownish or purplish skin, these are sweeter and less watery than regular onions. Sometimes known in Australia as eshallots or eschallots, these must not be confused with spring onions, widely and incorrectly called shallots in Australia.

SHRIMP PASTE, DRIED: A pungent seasoning used throughout Southeast Asia, this should be available in any Asian store.

SICHUAN PEPPER: The reddish brown berry of the prickly ash or fagara tree, used primarily in Sichuan Chinese cuisine.

STAR ANISE: This Chinese spice resembles a flower with eight petals, each containing shiny brown seeds. Has a pronounced aniseed flavour.

TAMARILLO: An egg-shaped fruit with a dark red skin and orangey-red flesh with edible seeds. The tamarillo has an acid flavour and unique fragrance. No real substitute.

TURMERIC: Fresh turmeric is used in some Southeast Asian dishes and is available in many Australian markets; if this is not available, substitute 1 teaspoon of powdered turmeric for 2.5 cm (1 in) fresh turmeric.

WAKAME: A very popular seaweed in Japan, this is sold either dried or salted. Soak to soften before using. *Wakame* does not need cooking.

WARRIGAL GREENS: Known botanically as *Tetragonia,* this is a fleshy green-leafed plant native to Australia and New Zealand. It can be substituted with English spinach.

YABBY: A freshwater crustacean often found or reared in dams in Australia, this can be substituted with any crayfish or marine lobster.

Palm Sugar

Shallots

Warrigal Greens

Yabby

OYSTER CAPPUCCINO

Damien Pignolet, Bistro Moncur, Sydney

A superbly concentrated soup of oysters and mussel juice topped with whipped cream flavoured with a hint of the soup, this is served in a cup just like Australia's favourite form of coffee, cappuccino. Although it may be extravagant to prepare, the result is so sublime for those who love oysters that it's well worth while. If you do not want to open the oysters yourself and have an obliging fishmonger, make sure he reserves the juice that comes out of them as you will need it. Serves 6.

2 k (4 lb) mussels in the shell
¹/₂ cup dry white wine
100 g (3¹/₂ oz) short-grain rice
600 ml (20 fl oz) chicken stock
150 g (5 oz) fresh button mushrooms, caps and
stalks chopped
60 oysters in the shell
600 ml (20 fl oz) *crème fraîche*
freshly ground black pepper to taste
juice of 2 lemons
300 ml (10 fl oz) whipping cream

Clean the mussels and put in a large pan with the wine. Cover and cook until the mussels open. Strain the mussel juice through a cheesecloth or muslin and add sufficient water to make 600 ml (20 fl oz). Put the liquid into a clean saucepan, reserving the mussels for some other dish.

Add the rice and chicken stock to the saucepan, bring to the boil, cover and simmer until the rice is soft. Add the mushrooms and cook for another 10 minutes. Transfer to a blender and purée.

Open the oysters, taking care to keep the juices. Keep 12 oysters aside as a garnish and blend the remainder with about ¹/₄ cup of the puréed rice and mushroom mixture. Pass through a fine sieve into the balance of the purée. Remove 100 ml (3¹/₂ fl oz) of the purée and reserve.

Put the remaining purée in a pan and heat, working in the *crème fraîche*. Take care not to let the mixture boil. Adjust the seasoning with pepper and lemon juice; salt should not be necessary because of the saltiness of the mussel liquid.

Whip the cream stiffly and flavour it to taste with some or all of the reserved 100 ml (3¹/₂ fl oz) of purée. Divide the soup among six deep soup bowls, add two raw oysters per serving, top with a large spoonful of the whipped cream and grind some black pepper on top. Serve immediately.

YABBY AND ASPARAGUS SOUFFLE

Gerda Eilts, The Garden Restaurant, Parmelia Perth Hilton

A basic soufflé is lifted out of the ordinary with the inclusion of yabbies and asparagus. The baked soufflés are reheated in a cream sauce scented with tarragon and parmesan cheese. Serves 6.

18 raw yabbies or 18 medium-sized prawns, still in the shell
500 g (1 lb) green asparagus
75 g (2$\frac{1}{2}$ oz) butter
75 g (2$\frac{1}{2}$ oz) plain flour
$\frac{1}{2}$ cup chicken stock
$\frac{1}{2}$ cup milk
salt and pepper to taste
freshly grated nutmeg to taste
4 egg yolks, lightly beaten
6 egg whites
300 ml (10 fl oz) cream
1 heaped (Aus: 1) tablespoon chopped fresh tarragon
180 g (6 oz) gruyère cheese, grated

Opposite:
Plate by Alessi
from Ventura
Design, Lilyfield,
Sydney.

Bring a saucepanful of lightly salted water to the boil. Add the yabbies or prawns, return the water to the boil and immediately remove the pan from the heat. Stand for 5 minutes before removing the seafood. Drain the yabbies, peel, cut in half lengthwise and remove the intestinal tract. Keep the yabby or prawn halves aside and discard the shells.

Blanch the asparagus in lightly salted boiling water for 2 minutes, then drain. Cut and reserve the tips and cut the remaining asparagus pieces into 1 cm ($\frac{1}{2}$ in) pieces.

Melt the butter and add the flour, stirring gently for 2–3 minutes. Slowly add the chicken stock and milk and cook over very low heat for 10 minutes, stirring from time to time. Add salt, pepper and nutmeg to taste, then fold in the egg yolks. Add the asparagus pieces, reserving the tips.

Beat the egg whites stiffly and then fold a couple of spoonfuls into the sauce. Carefully fold in the remaining egg whites.

Lightly grease 6 ramekins or individual soufflé dishes with butter, then put 4 yabby or prawn halves into each. Fill each ramekin with the egg mixture. Stand the ramekins in a baking dish half-filled with water and bake in a moderate oven (180°C/350°F) for 20–25 minutes. Cool, unmould and set aside. The soufflés can be prepared several hours in advance.

Just before the soufflés are required, put each into a heatproof bowl and pour over some of the cream. Put 2 of the reserved yabby or prawn halves on top and scatter with a little fresh tarragon. Add gruyère cheese and bake at 180°C/350°F for 8 minutes. Serve immediately, garnished with the reserved asparagus spears.

TERRINE OF RABBIT WITH PRUNES

Damien Pignolet, Bistro Moncur, Sydney

2 wild rabbits with livers or 1 farmed rabbit, about 1.5 k (3 lb)
2 tablespoons Armagnac
1 teaspoon coarsely ground black pepper
3 teaspoons fresh thyme leaves
400 g (13 oz) pork shoulder
400 g (13 oz) pork back fat
1 teaspoon oil
1 small onion, finely diced
1 large clove garlic, chopped
1 teaspoon *quatre épices* (page 134)
2 tablespoons white wine
1 bay leaf
1 egg
2 tablespoons finely chopped parsley
12–14 prunes, stones removed
rabbit stock (page 134)

Remove all the flesh from the rabbits, reserving one of the loin fillets in one piece. Put the fillet in a dish and moisten with a little of the armagnac, some of the pepper and a pinch of the thyme leaves. Cover and chill. Reserve the rabbit livers. Use the bones to make the stock (page 134).

Dice the rabbit meat, pork shoulder and pork fat roughly. Heat the oil in a small pan and sauté the diced onion until it turns transparent. Add the garlic, remaining pepper, thyme and *quatre épices.* Add the white wine, remaining armagnac and bay leaf. Mix well, cover and chill for 4 hours.

Transfer the mixture to a bowl. Add the egg, chopped parsley, chopped reserved rabbit livers and salt. Beat well until firm.

Grease a terrine with a little softened butter. Put in one-quarter of the minced mixture and press the top down firmly with the back of a spoon. Put a layer of half the prunes down the centre of this and top with another quarter of the mixture, pressing down firmly. Lay the rabbit fillet on the centre of this and add another quarter of the mixture. Put the remaining prunes over the top, add the final portion of rabbit and pork mixture and press the top. Tap the terrine firmly on the top of the bench, cover and refrigerate for 1 hour.

Put the terrine in a baking dish with hot water half-way up the sides of the terrine. Bake at 170°C/340°F for 30 minutes, then carefully pour off most of the fat. Pour in some or all of the stock to cover the meat. Cover and return the terrine to the oven for another 30–60 minutes. The terrine is cooked when the fatty liquids look clear and the mixture has begun to pull away from the sides. Remove from the oven and place a weight on top. Leave until cold, then remove the weight and refrigerate the terrine for at least 3 days before serving. If the top is sealed with melted pork fat, it will keep refrigerated for up to 2 weeks.

YAM AND MACADAMIA CROQUETTES

Beh Kim Un, Shakahari, Melbourne

Surprisingly simple to make, this crunchy, flavourful combination of steamed Asian tubers, macadamia nuts and seasonings can be served as an appetiser or feature as a main course for vegetarians. Tinned salted (pickled) mustard greens (known in Cantonese as *ham choy*) are available in any Chinese store.

Opposite:
*Table from
Arts of Asia,
Armadale,
Melbourne;
platter from Terry
Baker of Golden
Canvas Gallery,
Balmain, Sydney.*

$\frac{1}{3}$ cup vegetable oil
1 medium-sized onion, finely sliced
3 cloves garlic, very finely chopped
200 g (7 oz) roasted unsalted macadamia nuts, coarsely crushed
4 teaspoons (Aus: 1 tablespoon) dried chilli flakes
$\frac{1}{2}$ cup finely sliced long beans
$\frac{1}{2}$ cup finely sliced salted mustard greens
300 g (10 oz) yam, steamed until soft, peeled and mashed
150 g (5 oz) cassava (tapioca root) or potato, steamed until soft, peeled and mashed
4 teaspoons (Aus: 1 tablespoon) chopped palm sugar (preferably coconut)
scant 3 (Aus: 2) tablespoons rice flour
salt to taste
oil for shallow frying

Coriander Coconut Sauce:

6 fresh coriander plants (see below)
1–2 red chillies, finely sliced
$\frac{1}{2}$ cup lemon juice
2 cups water
2 cloves garlic, sliced
100 g ($3\frac{1}{2}$ oz) palm sugar (preferably coconut), chopped
$\frac{1}{2}$ cup toasted desiccated coconut
salt to taste

Heat the oil and gently stir fry the onion until transparent. Add the garlic and cook for a few seconds, then put in the macadamia nuts and chilli flakes. Stir fry for 2 minutes, then add the long beans and salted mustard greens. Stir fry for another 2 minutes, then add all remaining ingredients except oil, stirring to mix well. Transfer to a bowl and allow to cool.

Prepare the **coriander coconut sauce**. Finely chop the roots and 5 cm (2 in) of the coriander stems. Measure $\frac{1}{2}$ cup of coriander leaves and reserve the remainder for some other dish. Put the coriander roots and stems into a heavy bottomed pan, add the chillies, lemon juice, water, garlic and palm sugar. Cook, stirring from time to time, until the mixture has reduced by half. Transfer to a blender, add the coriander leaves and desiccated coconut and process to make a purée. Keep aside.

Just before the dish is required, shape the yam and macadamia mixture into small croquettes. Heat a little oil in a frying pan until very hot, then fry the croquettes on both sides until golden brown. Serve hot with the coriander coconut sauce.

4 teaspoons (Aus: 1 tablespoon) *mirin*
2 teaspoons sesame oil
2 teaspoons oyster sauce
freshly ground black pepper to taste

It is important to choose *sashimi* quality cuttlefish. Clean it thoroughly with a damp cloth, making sure there is no ink on it. Turn the cuttlefish so that the inside faces upwards and shave off the finest possible slices, using a very sharp knife. Gather together to make the shape of 6 roses. Cover and refrigerate until serving.

Put the cooked pasta in a bowl. Combine all other ingredients in a small bowl, mixing well, then pour over the noodles and toss to mix thoroughly. Divide the noodles into small portions and top each with a "white rose" of raw cuttlefish.

OCTOPUS IN AIOLI

2 kg (4 lb) octopus tentacles
200 ml (7 fl oz) olive oil
40 g (1¼ oz) black olives, crushed (stones left in)
4 cloves garlic, crushed
¼ bay leaf
½ red chilli
4 teaspoons (Aus: 1 tablespoon) lemon juice
6 parsley stalks

Aioli:

6 cloves garlic
1 red chilli, sliced
4 fresh coriander roots, washed and chopped
1 teaspoon sea salt
1 egg yolk

100 ml (3½ fl oz) olive oil
4 teaspoons (Aus: 1 tablespoon) lemon juice

Peel the skin off the octopus but leave the suckers intact. Pat dry. Bring the oil to the boil, add the crushed olives and fry until the oil smokes; this should take about 15 minutes. Gently gather the small ends of the octopus tentacles and carefully lower into the hot oil to seal quickly. Take care as the oil will spatter. Reduce the temperature to a minimum and add all other ingredients. Cover the pan and simmer gently for 35–40 minutes. The octopus should then be as soft as cooked lobster meat.

Make the **aioli** by pounding the garlic, chilli, coriander roots and salt together to make a fine smooth paste. This will require patience and time. Put the egg yolk and pounded mixture into a bowl and whisk with a fork. Slowly add the olive oil, drop by drop at first, whisking constantly to emulsify and create a smooth mayonnaise. Add salt and lemon juice to taste and set aside.

To serve, cut the cooked octopus tentacles into 1 cm (½ in) lengths, each with a sucker. Arrange on a plate with a little of the aioli spooned over the top. Garnish if liked with slivers of peeled tomato flesh and a sprig of fresh coriander.

SPICED PRAWN WITH GLUTINOUS RICE SUSHI

6 raw king or tiger prawns, shelled and deveined
a pinch of salt
a pinch of sugar
a pinch of finely grated lime peel
1 teaspoon tamarind pulp, soaked in scant 3 (Aus: 2) tablespoons warm water and

strained for juice
scant 3 (Aus: 2) tablespoons chopped palm
    sugar (preferably coconut)

Spice Paste:

3 teaspoons dried shrimp paste
5 cm (2 in) galangal
2 cm ($^{3}/_{4}$ in) fresh turmeric
5 cm (2 in) ginger
6–10 shallots
3 cloves garlic
1 red chilli
6 candlenuts or raw macadamia nuts
4 (Aus: 3) tablespoons peanut oil
scant 3 (Aus: 2) tablespoons coconut cream

Glutinous Rice Sushi:

200 g (7 oz) glutinous white rice
2 teaspoons sea salt
4 teaspoons (Aus: 1 tablespoon) peanut oil
$5^{1}/_{2}$ (Aus: 4) tablespoons coconut cream
30 x 20 cm (12 x 8 in) piece of banana leaf,
    stems and hard edges discarded

Cut the prawns in half lengthwise. Sprinkle with salt, sugar and lime peel and refrigerate.

To make the **glutinous rice sushi**, soak the rice in cold water for 1 hour. Strain and mix with the salt and oil. Spread out on a plate and steam in a steaming basket set over a wok of boiling water for 15–20 minutes. Put in a bowl and stir in coconut cream.

To make the banana leaf pliable, hold over a gas flame, turning until it softens. Alternatively, plunge in boiling water for a few seconds. Lay it flat and spread the cooked rice in a log shape 24 cm ($9^{1}/_{2}$ in) wide across the centre. Roll up the banana leaf, tucking in the edges, to make a roll about 3–4 cm ($1^{1}/_{4}$–$1^{1}/_{2}$ in) in diameter. Wrap this roll in aluminium

foil and grill over charcoal for about 15 minutes, turning so that the roll cooks on all sides. When unwrapped, the rice roll will be slightly brown and permeated with the wonderful fragrance of the banana leaf.

Prepare the **spice paste**. Wrap the dried shrimp paste in foil and cook under a grill or place in a pan and cook over moderate heat for about 3–4 minutes, turn and cook the other side. Crumble the cooked shrimp paste into a blender. Chop all other spice paste ingredients (except the oil and coconut cream) and add to the blender. Process to obtain a fine paste, adding a little of the oil if necessary to keep the blades turning.

Heat the remaining oil in a wok and add the ground spice paste together with the coconut cream. Stir fry on low heat until the mixture smells fragrant and the oil starts to separate.

Add the prawns, tamarind juice and palm sugar and cook, stirring from time to time, until the prawns are done.

To serve, cut the glutinous rice *sushi* into 6 pieces each 4 cm ($1^{1}/_{2}$ in) in length. Stand upright and place a spiced prawn on top of each. If liked, garnish with a sprig of fresh coriander leaf and a little very finely shredded cucumber.

TEA-SMOKED TUNA WITH SWEET-SOUR FENNEL SALAD

Christine Manfield, The Paramount Restaurant, Sydney

The Chinese tea-smoking method is used for tuna in this appetiser, which serves 6.

6 pieces 2 cm ($^3/_4$ in) thick belly tuna, weighing about 125 g (4 oz) each
4 (Aus: 3) tablespoons tea smoking mixture (page 134)
1 long thin cucumber, about 2.5–3 cm (1–1$^1/_4$ in) in diameter
1 cup (tightly packed) very finely sliced fennel bulb
scant 3 (Aus: 2) tablespoons very finely diced red onion
scant 3 (Aus: 2) tablespoons pickled ginger slices, sliced in fine shreds
2 small Asian aubergines (eggplants), roasted, peeled and sliced
2 teaspoons basil leaves, finely sliced
12 small raddichio leaves
18 Belgian endive leaves
sweet and sour dressing (page 135)

Line a large wok with foil and place over high heat. While the wok is heating, lay a sheet of baking paper across a steaming basket that fits neatly over the wok. Pierce the paper in several places around the outside with a skewer to allow the smoke to circulate. Lay the tuna pieces on the paper, making sure they do not touch. It may be necessary to do 2 batches to ensure even smoking.

Spread the prepared tea-smoking mixture over the foil in the base of the wok. When this starts to heat and burn at the edges, place the tuna-filled steaming basket over the top and cover with a tight-fitting lid. (Do this under an exhaust vent to avoid filling your kitchen with smoke.) Smoke the tuna for 4 minutes, remove the lid and turn the tuna over. Replace the lid and smoke for another 2 minutes. It must not be smoked for too long as this produces a high tannin content and bitter taste. Remove the steamer from the wok immediately. Wrap up the burnt remains of the tea-smoking mixture in the foil and discard.

Take the tuna out of the steamer and leave until it is cool enough to handle. Slice the tuna along the grain, then cut into dice. It should be cooked on the outside and very pink and rare in the centre.

Peel the cucumber and shave into long strips with a vegetable peeler, discarding the core of seeds. Put the cucumber and fennel slices in half of the sweet and sour dressing for 3 minutes.

Combine the smoked tuna and aubergine in the remaining sweet and sour dressing and marinate for 1 minute. Combine the marinated cucumber and fennel with the tuna and aubergine and add all other ingredients, mixing carefully to ensure even distribution. Pile on 6 serving plates and serve immediately. (This salad should not be chilled.)

TURKEY SALAD WITH TAMARILLO AND MANGO

Kurt Looser, San Francisco Grill, Sydney Hilton

The intense flavour and acidity of the tamarillo, a deep red, egg-shaped fruit which used to be known in some countries as the tree tomato, provides a contrast to the sweetness of fresh mango in this quickly prepared turkey salad.

Opposite:
*Salad servers
from Orson &
Blake Collectibles,
Woollahra,
Sydney; salad
bowl from
David Hislop,
Paddington
Bazaar, Sydney;
glassware and
pewter bowl
from Mexico,
Paddington,
Sydney.*

4 tamarillos, blanched in boiling water, peeled and sliced
2 ripe mangoes, peeled and sliced
8–10 leaves butter lettuce
8 leaves green oak leaf lettuce
4 leaves red leaf (coral) lettuce
250 g (8 oz) smoked turkey roll, thinly sliced
1 heaped (Aus: 1) tablespoon toasted almond flakes

Dressing:

120 ml (scant 4 fl oz) almond, hazelnut or walnut oil
2$\frac{1}{2}$ (Aus: 2) tablespoons white wine vinegar
5$\frac{1}{2}$ (Aus: 4) tablespoons crushed almonds
salt and pepper to taste

Combine all the **dressing** ingredients, mixing well.

Arrange the sliced mangoes and tamarillos in the centre of a large platter, or on 4 individual salad plates. Toss the butter and green oak lettuce with a little of the dressing and arrange on top of the fruit. Arrange slices of smoked turkey on top and garnish with the red leaf lettuce. Sprinkle with more dressing and scatter the almonds on top.

LETTUCE AND FRIED SQUID WITH BLACK-BEAN DRESSING

Herbert Franceschini, Victoria's Restaurant, Brisbane Hilton

A mixture of small lettuce leaves makes a bed for deep-fried squid dressed with an East-West dressing where Chinese black beans, soy sauce and sesame oil are partnered with European olive oil and balsamic vinegar.

300 g (10 oz) small lettuce leaves such as rocket, chicory, romaine, frisée, oak leaf lettuce, butter lettuce
1 small to medium red capsicum (bell pepper)
750 g (1½ lb) small fresh squid
2 cups plain flour
1 teaspoon salt
1 teaspoon freshly ground black pepper
4 teaspoons (1 tablespoon) paprika
olive oil for deep frying

Black-bean Dressing:

1 clove garlic, lightly bruised
5 tablespoons plus 1 teaspoon (Aus: 4 tablespoons) balsamic vinegar
¼ teaspoon salt
a little freshly ground black pepper
1 teaspoon black-bean and chilli sauce (available tinned from Chinese stores)
1 teaspoon fermented black beans, rinsed and finely chopped
pinch of sugar
scant 3 (Aus: 2) tablespoons sesame oil
scant 3 (Aus: 2) tablespoons olive oil
5 tablespoons plus 1 teaspoon (Aus: 4 tablespoons) light soy sauce

Opposite:
Glass platter by Natasha Fogel, Balmain Market, Sydney.

Prepare the **black-bean dressing** in advance by putting the garlic in a jar with the vinegar, salt and pepper. Set aside for several hours to allow the flavours to amalgamate. Discard the garlic and add black-bean and chilli sauce, chopped black beans and sugar. Slowly whisk in both lots of oil. Store at room temperature until required.

Wash the lettuce leaves and dry thoroughly. Wrap in a clean towel and refrigerate until required.

Cut the capsicum into fine julienne shreds and put in a bowl of iced water. Leave in the fridge for about 1 hour until they curl.

Peel the skin off the squid, clean thoroughly and dry with kitchen paper. Cut the squid into rings; if liked, trim off the long straggling ends of the squid tentacles, and discard the top beaky portion. Combine the flour, salt, pepper and paprika in a plastic bag. Add some of the squid rings (and the tentacles if using) and shake in the bag to coat with the flour. Lift the squid out and shake in a sieve or colander to dislodge excess flour. Repeat with the remaining squid.

Heat the oil until very hot and deep fry the squid, a little at a time, until golden brown. Drain.

Toss the lettuce leaves with the prepared dressing and serve with the squid placed on top. Garnish with the capsicum curls.

CRAB TORTELLI

Bill Marchetti, Marchetti's Latin, Melbourne

3 k (6 lb) live mud crabs
12 cups (3 litres) water
300 ml (10 fl oz) dry white wine
500 g (1 lb) of mixed celery, carrot, and onion, chopped
4 bay leaves
handful of parsley stalks
1 teaspoon black peppercorns
scant 3 (Aus: 2) tablespoons salt
handful of fennel tops (optional)
50 g (1½ oz) butter
½ cup very finely diced onion
béchamel sauce (page 135)
4 teaspoons (Aus: 1 tablespoon) chopped parsley
scant 3 (Aus: 2) tablespoons grated parmesan
pinch of cayenne pepper
salt and pepper to taste
pasta dough (page 136)
2 egg yolks, stirred
butter sauce (page 136)
scant 3 (Aus: 2) tablespoons finely chopped chives
freshly ground black pepper

Place the crabs in the freezer for a couple of hours to kill them. Put the water, wine, chopped vegetables, bay leaves, parsley, pepper, salt and fennel tops into a very large saucepan and bring to the boil. Cover, lower the temperature and simmer for 30 minutes. Add the crabs, bring the liquid back to the boil and simmer the crabs for 20 minutes. Remove the crabs from the pan and allow to cool for an hour before extracting the meat and discarding all traces of cartilage. Chop 400 g (13 oz) of the crab meat and save the remainder for garnish.

Heat the butter in a heavy pan and sauté the chopped onion until transparent. Add the chopped crab meat and sauté for 2 minutes. Add the béchamel sauce, parsley, parmesan cheese, cayenne pepper, salt and pepper, mixing well. Turn the mixture onto a greased plastic tray and cover with buttered greaseproof paper.

Cut circles of pasta dough with a 6 cm (2½ in) cutter. Brush the edge of one circle with the stirred egg yolks and place a soup spoon full of the crab mixture in the centre. Place another circle of dough on top and press around the edges. Repeat until all the circles of dough are used up. Place the tortelli in a single layer on a flat tray covered with greaseproof paper.

Bring a large pan of salted water to the boil and add the tortelli. Cook for about 5 minutes. Check one tortelli, making sure the edges where it has been sealed are thoroughly cooked. Remove the tortelli carefully with a slotted spoon, drain and toss in the butter sauce. Sprinkle with chopped chives, black pepper and reserved crab meat and serve immediately.

RAVIOLI OF LOBSTER WITH TOMATO AND BASIL

Tetsuya Wakuda, Tetsuya's, Sydney

These delicate ravioli are stuffed with lobster and scallops, although a combination of prawns and good quality white fish could be used if preferred. It is important to chill the seafood and cream thoroughly before making the ravioli filling.

200 g (7 oz) raw scallops or peeled raw prawns, chilled
$\frac{1}{3}$ teaspoon finely chopped fresh tarragon
4 teaspoons (Aus: 1 tablespoon) finely chopped chives
1 egg white
300 ml (10 fl oz) cream, chilled
salt and black pepper to taste
200 g (7 oz) cooked lobster meat or white fish fillet, finely diced and chilled
24 *gow gee* or *won ton* wrappers
24 x 2 cm ($\frac{3}{4}$ in) squares toasted laver (*nori*)
Japanese seaweed *(wakame* and *ogo*) to garnish
4 teaspoons flying fish roe or red lumpfish roe to garnish

Tomato and Basil Dressing:

100 ml ($3\frac{1}{2}$ fl oz) extra virgin olive oil
2 (Aus: $1\frac{1}{2}$) tablespoons rice vinegar
$\frac{1}{2}$ cup finely diced peeled tomato
1 teaspoon coriander powder
$\frac{1}{2}$ teaspoon finely chopped basil
$\frac{1}{4}$ teaspoon finely chopped garlic
salt and white pepper to taste
pinch of sugar

Chop the scallops or prawns coarsely and blend to a paste with the tarragon, chives and egg white, gradually adding the cream in a thin stream while the motor is still running. When the cream is incorporated, season with salt and pepper. Stir in the lobster or fish and leave to chill.

Prepare the **tomato and basil dressing** by stirring all ingredients together. Prepare the *wakame* and *ogo* seaweeds by rinsing and soaking separately in cold water for 10 minutes. Drain thoroughly and shred the *wakame* finely.

Lay out the *gow gee* or *won ton* wrappers and top each with a square of *nori*. Put a spoonful of the seafood filling in the centre of each. Wet the edges of the wrapper with a finger dipped in water and lay another piece of *gow gee* on top, pressing the edges gently to seal.

Bring a large saucepanful of salted water to the boil, then add the vegetable oil and ravioli. Lower the heat to just below boiling and gently simmer the ravioli for about 5 minutes; it is important not to let the water boil rapidly or it will spoil the texture and appearance of the ravioli. Drain the cooked ravioli.

Put some shredded *wakame* on the bottom of each plate, top with ravioli and pour over the prepared sauce. Garnish with a little *ogo* seaweed and 1 teaspoon of flying fish roe per serving.

CRAB SALAD ON BUCKWHEAT NOODLES

Stephanie Alexander, Stephanie's, Melbourne

Inspired by the refreshing chilled buckwheat noodles popular in Japan during summertime, this combination of seasoned crabmeat with dressed noodles makes an excellent starter to a meal.

250 g (8 oz) fresh crabmeat
200 g (7 oz) buckwheat noodles (*soba*)
4 teaspoons (Aus: 1 tablespoon) lemon juice
4 teaspoons (Aus: 1 tablespoon) extra virgin olive oil
4 teaspoons (Aus: 1 tablespoon) freshly chopped parsley
1 teaspoon black sesame seeds
scant 3 (Aus: 2) tablespoons chopped coriander leaves and fine stems

Dressing:
4 (Aus: 3) tablespoons light soy sauce
scant $1/2$ cup Chinese red rice vinegar
2 (Aus: $1^1/_2$) tablespoons sesame oil
2 (Aus: $1^1/_2$) tablespoons *mirin*
2 teaspoons very finely chopped ginger
2 teaspoons very finely chopped garlic
1 teaspoon very finely chopped red chilli

Vegetable Garnish:
1 leek, cut in 8 cm (3 in) long julienne shreds
1 carrot, cut in 8 cm (3 in) long julienne shreds
2 pieces of ginger, each 6 cm ($2^1/_2$ in) long, cut in julienne shreds
oil for deep frying

Pick over the crabmeat carefully, discarding any cartilage and shell. Reserve the crabmeat.

Bring a large saucepan of unsalted water to the boil and add the noodles. Stir to prevent them from sticking and after 4 minutes, add 1 cup of cold water and stir again until the water reboils. When the noodles are properly cooked (not firm or *al dente*), drain in a colander, rinse under cold running water and drain again.

Combine all **dressing** ingredients, mixing well, and moisten the cooked noodles with a little of this. Refrigerate the noodles until required.

Prepare the **vegetable garnish** by deep frying each vegetable separately in hot oil until crisp. Drain on paper towels. When all vegetables are cooked, mix together lightly and keep dry and warm.

To serve, season the crab with lemon juice, oil and parsley. Season the noodles with the sesame seeds, chopped coriander and plenty of the dressing. Coil a nest of noodles on each of 4 plates and place a mound of dressed crab on top.

Garnish with a topknot of vegetable garnish. If liked, deep-fried parsnip chips can be used as an additional garnish. (Stephanie's own Watermelon Rind Pickle is used as an additional garnish in the photograph.)

AUBERGINE WITH POLENTA AND BUSH TOMATO SALSA

Paul Hoeps, Breezes Restaurant, Cairns Hilton

An ideal dish for a vegetarian meal, alternating slices of polenta and aubergine are given extra flavour by a sauce made with native bush tomatoes. Sun-dried tomatoes make an acceptable substitute.

> 1 large aubergine (about 500 g/1 lb), cut cross-wise in 1 cm ($^1/_2$ in) slices, skin left on
> salt
> 1 cup milk
> $^1/_2$–1 cup olive oil
> bush tomato salsa (page 136)
> 4 (Aus: 3) tablespoons chopped basil
> 75 g ($2^1/_2$ oz) red capsicum (bell pepper), finely diced
> 75 g ($2^1/_2$ oz) sweet corn kernels
> 1 teaspoon chopped oregano
> 100 g ($3^1/_2$ oz) mozzarella cheese, sliced
> 12 whole basil leaves, deep fried until crisp

Polenta:

> 100 g ($3^1/_2$ oz) fine polenta
> 2 cups milk
> 1 clove garlic, very finely chopped
> 2 teaspoons grated parmesan cheese
> 4 egg yolks

Prepare the **polenta** first by combining the polenta, milk and garlic in a saucepan (preferably non-stick). Bring to the boil and simmer, stirring constantly, for 10 minutes. Stir in the cheese, remove from heat and allow to cool slightly. Beat in the egg yolks and spread on a waxed-paper-lined 20 x 30 cm (8 x 12 in) baking dish. Leave to set.

Salt the sliced aubergine liberally and leave in a colander for 30 minutes. Rinse under running water and soak in milk for 10 minutes. Heat $^1/_4$ cup of the olive oil and fry the aubergine slices on both sides until golden brown. Add a little more oil if necessary.

Cut the polenta into circles the same size as the aubergine slices. Put a polenta slice on a baking dish greased with a little olive oil. Top with a table-spoonful of the bush tomato salsa and a slice of fried aubergine. Sprinkle with a little chopped basil and add another slice of polenta, some more salsa and another slice of fried aubergine. Top with a slice of mozzarella. Repeat until all the polenta and aubergine is used up. Bake in a moderate oven (180°C/350°F) for 10 minutes.

While the polenta and aubergine are baking, heat 1 tablespoon of the remaining olive oil and sauté the capsicum, sweet corn and oregano until the capsicum is tender.

To serve, put a tower of polenta and aubergine in the centre of each plate and garnish with the sautéd capsicum and sweet corn. Top with deep-fried basil leaves.

SNAPPER AND PRAWN MOUSSE IN NORI OMELETTE

Christine Manfield, The Paramount Restaurant, Sydney

600 g (1¹/₄ lb) snapper fillet, skinned and
    boned
prawn mousse (page 137)
2 bunches English spinach, washed, stems
    removed and leaves blanched
40 g (1¹/₄ oz) unsalted butter
sea salt to taste
freshly ground black pepper to taste
prawn sauce (page 137)
6 teaspoons fresh salmon eggs

Nori Omelettes:

3 large eggs
¹/₂ teaspoon sesame oil
¹/₂ teaspoon fish sauce
pinch of freshly ground black pepper
pinch sea salt
1 large sheet of toasted laver (*nori*), cut in 1
    cm (¹/₂ in) strips

Prepare the **nori omelettes** first. Whisk the eggs lightly, then add the sesame oil, fish sauce, pepper and salt. Gently stir in the *nori* strips with a fork. Heat a 15 cm (6 in) non-stick pan over medium heat and brush the base of the pan with oil. Add just enough of the omelette mixture to coat the base of the pan, and cook until it begins to set. Remove the omelette and place on a flat surface. Repeat until the mixture is used up and you have 6 omelettes, stacking them on top of each other as they cook. Cover with a kitchen cloth until ready to use.

Slice the snapper fillets into thin even slices and lay carefully over the 6 omelettes. Spread the prawn mousse across the snapper in a thick horizontal line and roll up each omelette. Cover with cling film, rolling up like a sausage and keeping airtight, twisting the ends to keep firm. Rest in the fridge on a flat tray for 2 hours before cooking.

To cook the omelette-wrapped mousse, place in a steaming basket in a single layer, cover with a lid and steam over gently simmering water for 30 minutes, until the mousse is cooked and firm to the touch. Be sure to keep the water simmering only very gently as higher heat creates more steam which will cause the mousse to over-cook and explode out of the omelette covering. When the mousse is cooked, remove from the steamer and rest on a board for 2 minutes. Remove the cling film carefully and slice each omelette in half across the middle.

Heat the blanched spinach in the butter in a pan until warm, then season with a little salt and pepper and spoon onto the centre of the serving plates. Sit 2 omelette halves on the spinach with the cut side facing up, and ladle some of the hot prawn sauce around the base. Put ¹/₂ teaspoonful of salmon eggs in the centre of each omelette half and serve immediately. This recipe serves 6 as an appetiser.

BARRAMUNDI WITH BOK CHOY AND LAKSA SAUCE

Allan Koh, Chinois, Melbourne

Australia's excellent fine white-fleshed barramundi fish is steamed with baby Chinese *bok choy* cabbage and served with a spicy Malaysian *laksa* sauce, a reduction of the gravy that normally accompanies the popular noodle dish referred to as *laksa* in that country and in Singapore. Be sure to use only the finest quality fresh fish.

500 g (1 lb) barramundi or other white fish fillets, cut in 12 pieces
6 baby Chinese *bok choy* cabbage, halved lengthwise

Laksa Sauce:

$^1/_2$ **red onion, chopped**
1 lemon grass, use bottom 10 cm (4 in) only, finely sliced
2 cm ($^3/_4$ in) piece of fresh galangal, chopped
$^1/_2$ **dried red chilli, sliced and soaked to soften**
$^1/_4$–$^1/_2$ **cup oil**
1 teaspoon curry powder for fish
$^1/_4$ **teaspoon turmeric powder**
$^1/_4$ **teaspoon coriander powder**
$^1/_4$ **teaspoon cumin powder**
$^1/_4$ **teaspoon paprika**
$^1/_4$ **teaspoon dried shrimp paste**
$^1/_2$ **cup coconut milk**
$^1/_4$ **cup fish stock**
$^1/_2$–1 **teaspoon sugar, to taste**
$^1/_4$–$^1/_2$ **teaspoon salt, to taste**

Prepare the **laksa sauce** first. Put the onion, lemon grass, galangal and chilli in a blender and process until fine, adding a little of the oil if necessary to keep the blades turning. Heat the remaining oil in a saucepan and sauté the ground ingredients over moderate heat until fragrant; this should take 3–5 minutes. Add the curry powder, turmeric, coriander, cumin, paprika and shrimp paste and continue sautéing until the mixture smells fragrant. Slowly stir in the coconut milk, then add the fish stock and heat through. Season to taste with sugar and salt, and keep aside.

On a heatproof dish, alternate pieces of the fish and halves of the *bok choy*, overlapping slightly. Put inside a steamer and cook over boiling water for about 5–7 minutes, until cooked but not mushy and overcooked. (There is no need to season the fish as the *laksa* sauce will add flavour later.)

When the fish is cooked, gently reheat the *laksa* sauce but do not allow it to boil. Pour around the fish and *bok choy* and serve immediately.

ROAST YABBIES WITH APPLE AND CIDER SAUCE

Stephanie Alexander, Stephanie's, Melbourne

The succulent sweetness of Australia's fresh-water crayfish or yabbies is enhanced by a sauce made with cider, apples and butter.

12 yabbies, about 150 g (5 oz) each, or small crayfish or slipper lobster
handful of salt
4 teaspoons (Aus: 1 tablespoon) extra virgin olive oil
freshly ground black pepper
1 teaspoon fresh thyme leaves

Apple and Cider Sauce:
1 cup dry apple cider
1 cup cider vinegar
4 shallots or 2 pickling onions, finely chopped
1 bay leaf
1 sprig fresh thyme
4 teaspoons (Aus: 1 tablespoon) extra virgin olive oil
2 Golden Delicious apples, peeled, cored and cut in 1 cm ($^1/_2$ in) dice
1 tablespoon cream
150 g (5 oz) unsalted butter, cut in chunks
scant 3 (Aus: 2) tablespoons peeled, diced tomato (1 cm/$^1/_2$ in dice)
4 teaspoons (Aus: 1 tablespoon) freshly chopped parsley
salt to taste

Bring a large pot of salted water to the boil and put in the yabbies for 1 minute. Remove the yabbies and cool in iced water to stop further cooking. Drain well and split each yabby lengthwise. Remove the bony head sack and intestinal thread running down the centre. Paint the flesh with olive oil, sprinkle with thyme leaves and grind over black pepper. Arrange on a baking tray and refrigerate until required.

Make the **apple and cider sauce** by bringing the cider, cider vinegar, shallots, thyme and bay leaf to the boil in a stainless steel saucepan. Simmer until most of the liquid has evaporated, then strain.

Heat the olive oil in a non-stick pan and sauté the diced apples until lightly coloured. Keep warm.

Reheat the strained sauce and add the cream and heat until it simmers. Whisk in the butter piece by piece fairly quickly, adding the next piece before the previous one has completely melted. Remove from the heat and add the sautéd apples, diced tomato and parsley. Taste for seasoning, adding salt; it may be necessary to add a few drops of cider vinegar to balance the sauce at this point.

To cook the yabbies, put them on the oven tray into a very hot oven pre-heated to 250°C/475°F. Cook for 5 minutes, then transfer the yabbies to warmed plates and spoon the sauce around.

The yabbies can be garnished with some cooked green vegetable such as spinach, or, if it is obtainable, a little samphire.

CHICKEN BREAST AND PRESERVED LEMON COUSCOUS

Andrew Blake, Blake's, Melbourne

North Africa and Middle Eastern ingredients such as couscous, pomegranate seeds and preserved lemons make an excellent accompaniment to this deceptively simple chicken dish, served with rich pistachio butter.

4 **double chicken breasts**
3 **teaspoons olive oil**
2 **shallots, finely minced**
2 **cloves garlic, finely minced**
1$\frac{1}{2}$ **cups boiling chicken stock**
1$\frac{1}{2}$ **cups couscous**
$\frac{1}{4}$ **cup fresh pomegranate seeds**
$\frac{1}{4}$ **cup finely diced preserved lemon**
deep-fried julienne of leeks or parsnips to garnish (optional)

Pistachio Butter:

50 g (1$\frac{1}{2}$ oz) **unsalted raw pistachio nuts**
1 **bird's-eye chilli**
160 g (5$\frac{1}{2}$ oz) **unsalted butter**
$\frac{1}{4}$ **cup chopped parsley**
salt and pepper to taste

Opposite:
Red Coolibah wood platter by Rex Bailey of Golden Canvas Gallery, Balmain, Sydney.

Prepare the **pistachio butter**. Put the pistachio nuts and chilli on a dry tray and roast in a low to moderate oven (160°C/325°F) until lightly browned. Allow to cool, then rub off any skins that may be clinging to the nuts. Put the nuts and chilli into a food processor and pulse a few times until finely chopped but not mealy. Transfer to a bowl and add the parsley and butter. Mix thoroughly, adding salt and pepper to taste.

Heat the olive oil in a saucepan and gently sauté the shallots and garlic for about 5 minutes. Add the chicken stock and remove from heat. Put the couscous into a bowl and pour over the hot stock. Leave aside for 10 minutes, until the couscous has absorbed all the liquid and swollen. Use a fork to stir in the pomegranate seeds and preserved lemons. Check the seasoning, adding salt and pepper if necessary.

Grill the chicken breasts over charcoal, taking care not to overcook them. Reheat the couscous (a microwave oven is best for this). Divide the couscous between 4 plates, then add a piece of chicken to each and top with a dollop of pistachio butter. Garnish if liked with deep-fried julienne of leeks or parsnips.

FILLET OF VEAL WITH SEA URCHIN AND WASABI BUTTER

Tetsuya Wakuda, Tetsuya's, Sydney

The chef's Japanese origins are evident in the unusual flavouring of the butter which accompanies grilled veal or beef. If fresh sea urchin roe is not available, look for sea urchin paste in a jar in any Japanese food store.

8 veal medallions, or pieces of fillet beef steak, each weighing 80–100 g (2$^1/_2$–3$^1/_2$ oz)
2 teaspoons olive oil
4–5 tablespoons soaked and shredded Japanese *wakame* seaweed, to garnish
4–5 tablespoons Japanese *hijiki* seaweed, simmered in water and soy sauce, to garnish

Sea Urchin and Wasabi Butter:

6$^1/_2$ (Aus: 5) tablespoons Japanese horseradish (*wasabi*) powder
250 g (8 oz) unsalted butter, diced
60 g (2 oz) fresh sea urchin roe or 30 g (1 oz) sea urchin paste
scant 3 (Aus: 2) tablespoons finely chopped chives
2 teaspoons finely chopped fresh tarragon
$^1/_2$ teaspoon finely chopped fresh thyme
scant 3 (Aus: 2) tablespoons light soy sauce
2 teaspoons lemon juice
pinch of cayenne pepper

Prepare the **sea urchin and wasabi butter** first by blending the dry *wasabi* powder with sufficient water to make a stiff paste. Put the butter into a food processor and blend until almost white, then add the *wasabi* with all other ingredients and process to mix well. Put the butter onto a foil sheet and roll to make a tube. Store in the freezer until required.

Brush the veal or beef on both sides with the oil and grill or pan fry until medium rare. Place 2 medallions per person on a plate and top with the butter, cut into thick slices. Put the butter-topped meat under a very hot grill and cook until lightly brown. Garnish with the prepared seaweeds.

LAMB CUTLETS, SHEPHERD'S PIE AND RATATOUILLE

Alla Wolf-Tasker, The Lakehouse, Daylesford, Victoria

600 g (1¼ lb) lamb leg meat, very finely
   minced
2 cloves garlic, very finely diced
4 sprigs fresh thyme, very finely chopped
2 sprigs rosemary, very finely chopped
salt and pepper to taste
12–18 lamb cutlets, trimmed
pork caul fat for wrapping the cutlets
   (see below)
1 egg, lightly beaten with 1 teaspoon water to
   make egg wash
shepherd's pie casing (page 138)
shepherd's pie filling (page 138)

Ratatouille:
¼ cup olive oil
2 onions, finely diced
2 cloves garlic, finely minced
4 medium-sized zucchini (courgette), finely
   diced
1 green capsicum (bell pepper), finely diced
300 g (10 oz) unpeeled aubergine (eggplant),
   finely diced
300 g (10 oz) ripe tomatoes, peeled, deseeded
   and diced
salt and pepper to taste

Combine the minced lamb leg, garlic, herbs, salt and pepper and mix well. Press this around both sides of each lamb cutlet. Gently spread out a piece of the pork caul fat. Cut into pieces large enough to enclose each cutlet and wrap carefully. Refrigerate.

Prepare the **ratatouille** by heating the oil. Gently sauté the onion and garlic until softened. Add the zucchini, capsicum and aubergine, and sauté for 2–3 minutes. Add the tomatoes, including any juice which may have come out during dicing. Cover and simmer for 12–15 minutes. Remove cover, cook rapidly for 2 minutes, then season to taste.

Place 6 well-greased circular metal rings at least 7 cm (2¾ in) high and 5 cm (2 in) in diameter on a greased oven tray. Press some of the shepherd's pie casing across the bottom and up the inside of each ring. Leaving the metal ring in position, fill the centre of each potato mould with some of the shepherd's pie filling. Cover with a layer of mashed potato. Brush the top with egg wash and refrigerate until required.

To finalise the dish, place the shepherd's pies in a hot (200°C/400°F) oven and bake for 15 minutes or until a skewer inserted in the centre comes out hot. Seal both sides of the caul-wrapped lamb cutlets in a little oil in a very hot pan, the transfer to a hot oven for 12 minutes for medium-rare meat.

Reheat the ratatouille. Use an egg slice to lift each shepherd's pie onto the centre of a warm plate. Run a knife around the inside of each mould and lift away the ring. Arrange the cooked cutlets around the pie and garnish with ratatouille. Serves 6.

POT-ROASTED BABY LAMB, ARTICHOKES AND POLENTA

Bill Marchetti, Marchetti's Latin, Melbourne

1 side (half) a baby lamb, or 1 saddle of lamb, weighing about 3 kg (6 lb)
salt and pepper to taste
300 ml (10 fl oz) olive oil
2 cups diced onion
4 teaspoons (Aus: 1 tablespooon) finely chopped garlic
3 sprigs fresh rosemary
8 anchovy fillets, chopped
400 ml (13 fl oz) dry white wine
juice of 2 lemons
10 whole fresh artichokes
2 cups meat stock
polenta (page 139)

Trim any excess fat from the lamb and discard. Using a heavy knife or cleaver, chop the meat into 5 cm (2 in) pieces, cutting through the bones and leaving them in. (If you have a co-operative butcher, ask him to do the task for you.) Season the meat with salt and pepper.

Heat 200 ml (7 fl oz) of the olive oil in a heavy frying pan and add the pieces of meat, spreading out so each piece touches the base of the pan. Cook over medium heat, turning so that the meat is golden brown all over. Transfer the browned lamb to a baking dish.

In the same pan in which the meat was browned, sauté the onion, garlic, rosemary and anchovies until the onions turns light golden. Deglaze with the white wine and pour this over the meat.

Put the lemon juice into a large bowl of cold water. Discard all but the last 10 cm (4 in) of each artichoke stalk. Discard the hard outer leaves and cut about 2 cm ($^{3}/_{4}$ in) off the top of each artichoke bulb. Cut in half lengthwise and immediately put into the water to prevent them from discolouring. Repeat until all the artichokes are prepared.

Heat the remaining 100 ml ($3^{1}/_{2}$ fl oz) olive oil in a large frying pan. Drain the artichokes, pat dry and fry in the hot oil, turning to cook all over. Transfer the artichokes to the baking dish holding the lamb.

Cook in a moderate oven (180°C/350°F) for about 45 minutes, until the lamb is tender. Keep adding a little of the meat stock and basting the lamb during cooking. When the meat is tender, remove the meat and artichokes and keep warm. Transfer the gravy from the roasting pan to a saucepan and simmer to reduce slightly. Remove any excess fat, check the seasoning and keep warm.

Grill the squares of polenta over a charcoal grill or under a gas or electric grill until they take colour and are thoroughly hot.

To serve, spread some of the lamb sauce on heated dinner plates, add pieces of lamb and artichoke and garnish with the grilled polenta.

LAMB WITH CHICK PEA CURRY, HARISSA AND NAAN

Bethany Finn, The Grange Brasserie, Adelaide Hilton

1 kg (2 lb) hogget or lamb loin
harissa (page 139)
2 large red capsicums (bell peppers)
chick pea curry (page 139)

Naan:
1 kg (2 lb) self-raising flour
2 eggs
1 cup milk
water as needed
scant 3 (Aus: 2) tablespoons oil
1 teaspoon salt
4 teaspoons (Aus: 1 tablespoon) black onion
  seeds or nigella (*kalonji*)
4 teaspoons (Aus: 1 tablespoon) fennel seeds
4 teaspoons (Aus: 1 tablespoon) white poppy
  seeds

Prepare the dough for the **naan** by sifting the flour into a large bowl. Whisk the eggs and milk together and add to the flour, mixing in enough water to made a soft dough. Knead in the oil and leave to rest for 3 hours.

Rub the loin of lamb with about 2 tablespoons (Aus: 1 heaped tablespoon) of the *harissa* and set aside while the oven is heating to 200°C/400°F.

Cook the whole capsicums on a very hot grill, turning so that the skin blisters on all sides. Put in a plastic bag for 5–10 minutes (this makes them easier to peel). Peel the skin, discard the seeds and membrane and purée the flesh with the remaining *harissa*. Keep aside as a garnish.

To finalise the cooking, sear the lamb loin on all sides in a little olive oil in a very hot pan. Transfer it to a baking dish and cook in a hot oven for about 10–15 minutes, depending on how well you like the meat cooked.

While the loin is roasting, roll out the *naan* dough, shape into small balls and flatten a little, pulling into a tear-drop shape. Sprinkle the top of each with a mixture of the black onion seeds, fennel seeds and white poppy seeds. Place the *naan* onto a hot oven tray and bake for 8–10 minutes at 200°C/400°F, until puffed and golden brown.

Serve the chick pea curry in the centre of a plate, topped by slices of lamb. Drizzle a little of the capsicum and *harissa* purée to one side and serve with the *naan*.

BEEF, DUCK LIVER, BOK CHOY AND BUNYA NUTS

Herbert Franceschini, Victoria's Restaurant, Brisbane Hilton

A true cross-cultural dish, this partners top quality beef steak with a triangle of puff pastry, Australia's native bunya nuts, Chinese white cabbage and duck liver marinated in a sweet and sour sauce.

8 duck livers
8 whole bunya nuts or chestnuts
200 ml (7 fl oz) beef stock
salt and pepper to taste
4 triangles of uncooked puff pastry
 (see below)
2 (Aus: 1½) tablespoons butter
4 baby Chinese white cabbage (*bok choy*),
 halved lengthwise and blanched in boiling
 water until just tender
4 pieces beef fillet, each 180 g (6 oz)
2–3 teaspoons vegetable oil

Marinade:
 ½ cup lemon juice
 scant 3 (Aus: 2) tablespoons sugar
 2 cloves garlic, crushed
 1 red chilli, sliced

Combine all **marinade** ingredients in a small saucepan and bring to the boil. Remove from the heat and allow to cool. When the marinade is cool, add the cleaned duck livers and refrigerate for 4–6 hours.

Boil the bunya nuts or chestnuts in plenty of water for 30 minutes or until tender when pierced with a skewer. Drain, and when cool enough to handle, cut in half and remove the bunya nut from the shell, if liked. If using chestnuts, remove from the shell and peel away the fine skin.

Put the beef stock in a small pan and boil until reduced to just 50 ml (1½ oz). Season to taste and add the whole bunya nuts or chestnuts. Reheat gently just before serving.

Buy commercially prepared puff pastry and roll it out until very thin, cutting it into triangles. Bake in a hot oven (200°C/400°F) until puffed and golden brown.

While the pastry is cooking, drain the marinated duck livers, pat dry and fry in the butter until cooked but still pink inside. Keep warm.

Season the beef with salt and pepper, brush with oil and grill to your liking. Leave the meat to stand in a warm place for 5 minutes before cutting each piece into 3 slices.

Place the beef on serving plates, adding the bunya nuts and sauce, the fried duck liver and the cooked *bok choy*, reheated in a little butter. Garnish with a triangle of puff pastry.

BAKLAVA OF DRIED FRUITS WITH MINT SYRUP

Dietmar Sawyere, Forty One Restaurant, Sydney

Inspired by the Greek baklava, which normally contains crushed nuts between layers of flaky filo pastry, this recipe also incorporates some of the dried fruits for which Australia is justifiably renowned.

> **1 cup coarsely chopped mixed dried fruit (apricots, cherries and pears)**
> **2 cups raw unsalted pistachios**
> **$\frac{1}{2}$ cup ground hazelnuts**
> **$\frac{1}{2}$ cup sugar**
> **1 teaspoon cinnamon powder**
> **5 tablespoons plus 1 teaspoon (Aus: 4 tablespoons) Grand Marnier**
> **9 sheets filo pastry**
> **150–200 g (5–7 oz) unsalted butter, melted**
> **$\frac{1}{3}$ cup diced dried fruit (same mixture as above)**
> **clotted cream or ice-cream to accompany**

Mint Syrup:
> **$\frac{1}{2}$ cup caster sugar**
> **$\frac{1}{2}$ cup water**
> **2 sprigs mint**

Blend the dried fruit, pistachios, hazelnuts, sugar, cinnamon and Grand Marnier in a food processor to achieve a coarse mixture. Do not over blend; there should be some texture to the filling.

Place a sheet of filo pastry on a large wooden board or tabletop and brush with some of the melted butter. Place a second sheet on top and brush again.

Repeat with a third sheet of pastry.

Spoon one-third of the filling onto the pastry and spread out to within 2 cm ($\frac{3}{4}$ in) of the edge. Starting at one end, roll up tightly and place on a well-buttered baking sheet. Brush with more melted butter.

Repeat this process with the remaining filo pastry, so you have a total of three filled rolls. Refrigerate the rolls for 30 minutes. Bake in a hot oven (200°C/400°F) for 10–15 minutes until golden brown.

While the pastry is baking, prepare the **mint syrup**. Combine the sugar, water and mint in a pan, bring to the boil and simmer for 2 minutes.

When the baklava rolls are golden, remove from the oven, place on a cooling rack over a plate and spoon over a little of the syrup while the baklava is still warm. Add the diced dried fruit to the remaining syrup and bring to the boil. Remove from heat and keep aside.

To serve, slice the baklava (preferably while still warm) and arrange on 4 serving plates. Spoon over some of the syrup with diced fruits and serve either with clotted cream or ice-cream. Grand Marnier or Poire William ice-cream go particularly well with the baklava.

PUMPKIN SCONES AND BANANA BREAD

Werner Kimmeringer, Cliveden Room, Melbourne Hilton

PUMPKIN SCONES

$\frac{1}{2}$ cup granulated sugar
$\frac{1}{2}$ cup water
150 g (5 oz) cooked pumpkin, cut in 1 cm
    ($\frac{1}{2}$ in) dice
$\frac{1}{4}$ cup caster sugar
30 g (1 oz) softened butter
375 g (12 oz) cooked, mashed pumpkin
    (preferably butternut variety)
1 egg
2$\frac{1}{2}$ cups self-raising flour
pinch of salt
$\frac{1}{4}$ teaspoon cinnamon powder
1 pinch freshly grated nutmeg
$\frac{1}{4}$–$\frac{1}{2}$ cup milk (see below)

Combine the granulated sugar and water together in a small saucepan and simmer, stirring from time to time, until a syrup forms. Cool and add the diced pumpkin. Leave to marinate for a minimum of 8 hours; the pumpkin can be left for up to 3 days.

Beat the caster sugar and butter together, then add the mashed pumpkin and mix well. Beat in the egg. Sift the flour, salt, cinnamon and nutmeg into the pumpkin mixture, then add $\frac{1}{4}$ cup of milk. If necessary, add more milk to make a soft but not sticky dough; the amount of milk required will depend on the dryness of the pumpkin. Drain the soaked diced pumpkin and add to the dough, turning the mixture out onto a floured surface. Knead lightly, then pat out to a thickness of 2 cm ($\frac{3}{4}$ in). Cut into rectangles or use a floured cookie cutter to cut 5 cm (2 in) diameter circles.

Place the scones on a greased tray and bake in a hot oven (200°C/400°F) for 12–15 minutes, until risen and golden brown. Serve while still warm with fresh whipped cream.

BANANA BREAD

275 g (9 oz) ripe bananas, mashed
275 g (9 oz) brown sugar
3 eggs, lightly beaten
pinch salt
140 ml (4$\frac{3}{4}$ fl oz) milk
70 ml (2$\frac{1}{4}$ fl oz) vegetable oil
275 g (9 oz) plain flour
1 teaspoon bicarbonate of soda (baking soda)
1$\frac{1}{2}$ teaspoons baking powder

Mix the bananas, brown sugar and eggs together. Add the salt to the banana mixture, then stir in the milk. Add the oil and continue stirring.

Sift the flour, bicarbonate of soda and baking powder together, then add to the banana mixture. Blend together in a cake mixer for 10 minutes; this is important to ensure that the banana bread will be light. Pour into a greased loaf pan 30 x 10 cm (12 x 3 in). Bake at 160°C (325°F) for 2 hours.

CANNOLI ALLA SICILIANA

Bill Marchetti, Marchetti's Latin, Melbourne

If you are unable to find the metal tubes for making cannoli in a specialist kitchen shop, use 10 cm (4 in) lengths of wooden dowelling about 2 cm (¾ in) in diameter. This recipe makes about 20 cannoli.

680 g (1 lb 6 oz) plain flour
160 g (5½ oz) unsalted butter, melted
4 whole eggs
4 additional egg yolks
1 cup dry Marsala
pinch of salt
4 cups (1 litre) olive oil
500 g (1 lb) pork lard (optional)
icing sugar

Ricotta Filling:

600 g (1¼ lb) ricotta cheese
100 g (3½ oz) mascarpone
150 g (5 oz) mixed glacé fruits, finely diced
about 100 ml (3½ fl oz) Maraschino
4 (Aus: 3) tablespoons castor sugar, or more to taste

Orange Sauce:

4 cups (1 litre) freshly squeezed orange juice
200 g (7 oz) caster sugar
100 ml (3½ fl oz) Grand Marnier
3 teaspoons corn flour mixed with a little cold water

Prepare the cannoli first. Put the flour into the bowl of an electric mixer, make a well in the middle and pour in the melted butter, 2 whole eggs (reserving 2 for later use) and 4 egg yolks. Add the Marsala and salt and mix the dough on medium speed for about 5 minutes, until the dough is elastic. Put dough into a covered bowl and refrigerate for 2 hours to firm.

To make the **orange sauce**, combine the juice, sugar and water in a saucepan and simmer over moderate heat until reduced to about half. Mix in the corn flour and water and cook, stirring, until the sauce thickens and clears. Strain and cool.

Mix the **ricotta filling** by combining the ricotta, mascarpone and fruits in a bowl. Add Maraschino and sugar to taste and set aside.

When the cannoli dough has rested for 2 hours, roll it out in a pasta machine until very thin. Cut into squares of 9 cm (3½ in). Put a cannoli rod diagonally across each square of dough and roll up, so that the diagonal points meet in the middle. Lightly beat the 2 remaining eggs and brush the edges of each cannoli with this to seal.

Heat the olive oil and pork lard together (the lard improves the texture). Fry the cannoli in the hot oil until light golden in colour. Remove, drain, and when cool, pull out the tubes or dowelling.

Use a piping bag to fill each cooled cannoli with the ricotta filling. Dust with icing sugar and serve with the orange sauce.

Opposite:
Cutlery and blue plate from Villeroy & Boch, French's Forest, Sydney; glass platter from David Hislop, Paddington Bazaar, Sydney.

PAVLOVA WITH SEASONAL FRUITS

Marieke Brugman, Howqua Dale Gourmet Retreat, Mansfield, Victoria

This classic dessert, named after a famous ballerina, is popular in both Australia and New Zealand.

12 egg whites
3 cups caster sugar
4 teaspoons (Aus: 1 tablespoon) cornflour
1 teaspoon white vinegar
winter or spring fruits: a mixture of peeled and diced papaya, rock melon, cantaloupe, pineapple and mango
summer or autumn fruits: raspberries, strawberries, loganberries, boysenberries or blueberries
1–2 teaspoons lime or lemon juice
caster sugar to taste

Crème Chantilly:

300 ml (10 fl oz) whipping cream
1 teaspoon pure vanilla essence
4 tablespoons (Aus: 3) caster sugar
10 large strawberries, puréed

Passionfruit Caramel:

1 cup sugar
4 tablespoons (Aus: 3) water
pulp from 6–8 passionfruit

Line two baking sheets with silicon baking paper. Using a saucer as a guide, draw 6 circles about 8–10 cm (3–4 in) in diameter on each piece of baking paper, to make 12 mini-pavlovas. Set aside.

In a food mixer with a balloon whisk attachment, beat the egg whites until they start to mount in volume. Add the vinegar and continue beating until stiff. Sift over the cornflour, add $1\frac{1}{2}$ cups of sugar and beat again until very stiff and glossy. Keep the beaters running and very quickly incorporate the remaining $1\frac{1}{2}$ cups of sugar, a little at a time.

Put the mixture into a large piping bag fitted with a plain 1 cm ($\frac{1}{2}$ in) nozzle. Following the circles drawn on the paper, pipe the mixture into neat discs about 6–8 cm ($2\frac{1}{2}$–3 in) high. Bake the pavlovas in a very low oven (100°C/200°F) for $1\frac{1}{4}$–$1\frac{1}{2}$ hours, until the exterior is very crisp.

Prepare either summer or winter fruits according to season. Toss with a little lemon juice and sugar.

Make the **passionfruit caramel** by dissolving the sugar in water. Bring to the boil and cook until it turns a dark mahogany colour. Immediately add the passionfruit pulp and put back over low heat to dissolve the caramel.

Whip together the cream, vanilla and sugar to make the *crème chantilly*, adding the puréed strawberries to one-third of the cream. To serve, put the pavlovas in the centre of a plate and surround with mixed fruit. At the last minute, spread the strawberry *crème chantilly* over the top of the pavlovas, add the passionfruit caramel and serve the remaining *crème chantilly* separately. Serves 12.

LEMON MYRTLE BAVAROIS WITH ROSELLA FLOWER JELLY

Andrew Fielke, Red Ochre Grill, Adelaide

Opposite:
*Spoon by Alessi
from Ventura
Design, Lilyfield,
Sydney.*

macadamia or any other nut oil for brushing
    the moulds
5 teaspoons powdered gelatine
120 ml (scant 5 fl oz) warm water
400 ml (13 oz) whipping cream
450 ml (14½ fl oz) milk
200 g (7 oz) sugar
10 lemon myrtle leaves, or 5–6 kaffir lime
    leaves, finely shredded
5 egg yolks

Rosella Flower Jelly:

300 g (10 oz) rosella flowers, or 1 cup puréed
    raspberry and rhubarb
200 g (7 oz) sugar
50 ml (1½ fl oz) lemon juice
500 ml water
5 teaspoons powdered gelatine
120 ml (scant 5 fl oz) warm water

Use the oil to brush 10–12 ring moulds, each about 6 cm (2½ in) in diameter and 10 cm (4 in) high. Alternatively, use small soufflé or ramekin dishes.

Sprinkle the gelatine over warm water and leave until it softens and swells. Whip the cream to soft peaks and refrigerate.

Bring the milk, sugar and lemon myrtle leaves to the boil. Remove the pan from the heat immediately and stand for 10 minutes.

Whisk the egg yolks and pour in the warm milk, whisking fast all the time. Put the pan containing the mixture over a larger saucepan containing rapidly boiling water. Continue whisking until a custard forms.

Remove from the heat and add the gelatine. Mix well, pour through a fine sieve into a bowl and stand it in iced water. Stir continuously until the mixture cools and just begins to thicken. Quickly fold in the whipped cream and pour into the oiled moulds or soufflé dishes, leaving about 1 cm (½ in) at the top for the jelly to be added. Keep in the refrigerator.

Prepare the rosella flower jelly by chopping the flower petals finely. Put the rosellas or raspberry and rhubarb purée in a pan with water, sugar and lemon juice. Bring to the boil, lower the heat and simmer for 5 minutes, skimming the surface frequently. Pour the mixture through a fine sieve, measure 2 cups and mix in the gelatine.

Allow the jelly mixture to cool to room temperature, then pour a layer over the top of the bavarois. Leave to set in the refrigerator.

LEMON CURD TART WITH CREAM

Bethany Finn, The Grange Brasserie, Adelaide Hilton

This rich egg custard with a tangy lemon favour is ideally accompanied by fresh Kangaroo Island cream, pure dairy cream from South Australia.

9 eggs
400 g (13 oz) sugar
1 teaspoon finely grated lemon rind
1 cup lemon juice, sieved
1 vanilla bean
1 cup Kangaroo Island or other fresh cream
icing sugar to garnish
additional thick cream to garnish

Pastry:

200 g (7 oz) butter
100 g (3½ oz) sugar
pinch of salt
1 egg
300 g (10 oz) plain flour

Prepare the **pastry** first by mixing butter, sugar and salt until well combined. Add the egg and mix again, then add the flour and knead until well combined. Take care not to over-knead or the pastry will become too elastic. Refrigerate for 1 hour, then roll out into a very thin circle. Thoroughly grease the bottom and sides of a 25 cm (10 in) pie plate with a removable base and carefully press in the circle of pastry so that it covers the bottom and the sides. Trim the top edge with a sharp knife. Do not let any cracks or holes form in the pastry, which must come right up the the top of the pie plate.

Refrigerate pastry for 15 minutes. Put a circle of aluminium foil into the centre and coming up the sides of the pastry and fill with beans or rice. Bake for 15 minutes in a moderate oven (180°C/350°F).

While the pastry is baking, make the filling by whisking together the eggs and sugar to mix well, but take care to avoid whipping any air into the eggs. Add the lemon rind and juice and stir to mix. Cut the vanilla bean in half and scrape out the seeds. Put these into the egg mixture and finally stir in the 1 cup of cream.

When the pastry has been baked for 15 minutes, remove from the oven and carefully pour in the lemon filling. Reduce the heat to 150°C/300°F and bake for 1 hour. By this time, the filling should be just set but still somewhat soft, like a jelly. Check by gently tapping the tin; if the centre is still runny, bake for another 5–10 minutes and test again.

When the tart is baked, cool and then refrigerate for 1 hour. Remove the base from the pie plate and slide the tart onto a serving plate. Dust with icing sugar to make an even layer on the top of the tart and place under a hot grill for a few moments until it becomes brown and caramelised. Serve with plenty of fresh cream.

STEAMED MACADAMIA AND BANANA PUDDING

Herbert Franceschini, Victoria's Restaurant, Brisbane Hilton

100 g (3$\frac{1}{2}$ oz) butter
120 g (scant 4 oz) sugar
4 eggs, separated
a few drops of vanilla essence
pinch of salt
100 g (3$\frac{1}{2}$ oz) vanilla sponge cake, dried and crumbled
100 g (3$\frac{1}{2}$ oz) lightly toasted unsalted macadamia nuts, chopped
50 g (1$\frac{1}{2}$ oz) banana, mashed
100 ml (3$\frac{1}{2}$ fl oz) cream
1 teaspoon lemon rind
scant 3 (Aus: 2) tablespoons lemon juice

Caramel Sauce:

200 g (7 oz) sugar
50 ml (1$\frac{1}{2}$ fl oz) hot water
200 ml (7 fl oz) cream

Chocolate Sauce:

125 ml (4 fl oz) cream
125 ml (4 fl oz) milk
4 teaspoons (Aus: 1 tablespoon) honey
150 g (5 oz) dark chocolate, grated

Sugar Bark:

$\frac{1}{2}$ cup caster sugar
1 teaspoon instant coffee granules

To make the **sugar bark**, put sugar into a dry heavy pan and cook, without any water, over very low heat until golden brown. Sprinkle coffee granules on a large sheet of paper and pour over the toffeed sugar, spreading it with the back of a spoon to make a thin layer. Leave to set.

Prepare the **caramel sauce** by putting the sugar and water into a pan and cooking until it turns golden brown. Heat the cream in a separate pan. When the sugar has caramelised, stir in the boiling cream. Transfer to a jug and leave to cool.

To make the **chocolate sauce**, bring the cream, milk and honey to the boil, then whisk in the grated chocolate until it dissolves. Set aside.

Prepare the pudding by whisking the butter with 45 g (1$\frac{1}{2}$ oz) of the sugar until fluffy. Whisk in the egg yolks, 1 at a time. In a separate bowl, whip the egg whites with the remaining sugar and salt until stiff. Fold one-third of this into the sugar and butter mixture, then fold in the remaining egg white. Fold in the cake crumbs, nuts and mashed banana, then fold in cream, lemon rind and juice.

Grease 4 timbales and sprinkle with a little additional sugar. Put in the pudding mixture and place the timbales into a baking dish with water to come halfway up the sides. Cover timbales with foil and bake at 170°C/340°F for 1 hour.

Unmould and serve surrounded by the two sauces. Break the sugar bark with your hands into large pieces and use as a garnish.

POT-ROASTED QUINCES

Maggie Beer, Pheasant Farm, Nuriootpa, South Australia

Quinces, popular in the past, seem to have almost disappeared from today's fruit shops. Maggie Beer is so enthusiastic about them that she has established a quince orchard and is trying to share her love of this fruit. Quinces have the remarkable property of turning from a pale yellow to gold and through to a deep red colour during long slow cooking, making them as decorative as they are delicious. This dish is best attempted at the beginning of the season, when the quinces hold their shape better.

6 whole quinces
6 cups water
4 cups sugar
4 (Aus: 3) tablespoons lemon juice

Rub the down off the skin of the quinces and wash the fruit well, but do not peel. Try to keep the leaves on the stem if the fruit was obtained with them.

Choose a heavy-bottomed pan with a tightly fitting lid. Add water and sugar and bring to the boil, then put in the whole quinces, cover the pan and simmer for up to 3 hours. It is important to turn the quinces 2 or 3 times during cooking so that the rich red colour flows right through to the core of the fruit. Add the lemon juice about 20 minutes before the end of cooking time to remove excess sweetness.

Turn the temperature down if the juices seem in danger of burning, using a simmering mat or heat diffuser if necessary towards the final stage of cooking. The liquid will reduce to a thick red syrup. Serve the quinces with a little of the syrup and *crème anglaise* (rich custard).

Supplementary Recipes

*These recipes are required for some of the main dishes, as indicated
by the page numbers on each supplementary recipe*

Quatre Epices • see page 42

3 teaspoons whole allspice
$^1/_2$ nutmeg, smashed
2 teaspoons whole cloves
2 cm ($^3/_4$ in) cinnamon stick

Combine the whole spices in a spice grinder or
coffee mill and blend until finely powdered. Sieve.

Rabbit Stock • see page 42

rabbit bones (see page 42)
1 medium onion, sliced
1 clove garlic, bruised
1 small carrot, diced
1 stalk celery, sliced
150 ml (5 fl oz) white wine
1 teaspoon salt
sprig of fresh thyme
parsley stalk and leaves
1 bay leaf

Combine the rabbit bones with all stock ingredients
in a pan. Add water to cover. Bring to the boil, cover
and simmer for 3 hours. Strain and reserve.

Tea-Smoking Mixture • see page 56

4 teaspoons (Aus: 1 tablespoon) Chinese black
    Oolong tea leaves
4 teaspoons (Aus: 1 tablespoon) Chinese
    jasmine tea leaves

Measurements

Measurements in this book are given in volume
as far as possible: 1 measuring **cup** contains
250 ml (roughly 8 fl oz); 1 **teaspoon** contains
5 ml, while 1 **tablespoon** contains 15 ml or
the equivalent of 3 teaspoons.

Australian readers please note that the standard **Australian tablespoon** is larger than the
international standard, containing 20 ml or 4
teaspoons; Australian tablespoon measurements are given in brackets after the standard
tablespoon in all recipes.

Where **metric measurements** are given, ap-
proximate imperial conversions follow in
brackets.

Servings

Unless otherwise stated, the recipes are de-
signed to serve 4 persons.

zest of 1 orange
2 pieces dried tangerine peel, broken
scant 3 (Aus: 2) tablespoons raw fragrant long-
    grain ("jasmine") rice
scant 3 (Aus: 2) tablespoons brown sugar
3 whole star anise
2 teaspoons Sichuan peppercorns
3 pieces cassia bark

Combine all ingredients and use as directed.

Sweet and Sour Dressing • see page 56

100 ml ($3\frac{1}{2}$ fl oz) vegetable oil
pinch of dried chilli flakes
2 small cloves garlic, finely sliced
60 ml (2 fl oz) light soy sauce
100 ml ($3\frac{1}{2}$ fl oz) cider vinegar
150 ml (5 fl oz) sugar syrup, made from equal
    parts of sugar and water

Gently heat the oil together with chilli flakes and
garlic over low heat until the garlic is golden; take
great care not to burn the garlic or it will be bitter.
Add all other dressing ingredients and bring to the
boil. Remove from the heat and allow to cool.

Dressing for Lentil Salad • see page 60

4 teaspoons (Aus: 1 tablespoon) reduced
    chicken stock
100 ml ($3\frac{1}{2}$ fl oz) double cream
120 ml (scant 4 fl oz) olive oil
verjus or lemon juice to taste
salt and pepper to taste

Prepare the dressing by mixing the chicken stock
and cream, slowly working in the oil. Acidulate to
taste with verjus or lemon juice and season well
with salt and pepper.

Ravioli Filling • see page 64

2 teaspoons olive oil
100 g ($3\frac{1}{2}$ oz) finely diced mixed vegetables
    (carrot, leek and celery)
meat from bodies and claws of 8 yabbies or 8
    prawns, cut in large cubes
salt and pepper to taste
100 g ($3\frac{1}{2}$ oz) fresh salmon, finely chopped

Heat the oil in pan and sauté the vegetables and
yabby meat for just 30 seconds. Season to taste with
salt and pepper and allow to cool before mixing in
the salmon.

Ravioli Dough • see page 64

250 g (8 oz) plain flour
3 whole eggs
1 additional egg yolk
4 teaspoons olive oil
4 teaspoons water
salt and white pepper to taste
1 teaspoon chopped parsley

Mix all the ingredients together in a food processor
or combine quickly by hand. Do not overwork the
dough; otherwise, it will become tough. Cover
with plastic until needed.

Béchamel Sauce • see page 68

1 cup milk
1 bay leaf
a little freshly grated nutmeg
scant 3 (Aus: 2) tablespoons butter
scant 3 (Aus: 2) tablespoons plain flour
salt and pepper to taste

Bring the milk to the boil together with the bay leaf
and nutmeg. Remove the pan from the heat. In a

separate saucepan, melt the butter over low heat and stir in the flour, mixing until smooth. Add the heated milk and whisk well. Season with salt and pepper and cook over low heat, stirring continously, for 10 minutes. Transfer the béchamel sauce to a bowl and cover the surface with a piece of buttered greaseproof paper to prevent a skin from forming.

Pasta Dough • see page 68

600 g (1¼ lb) strong plain flour (bread flour)
5 eggs, beaten
4 teaspoons (Aus: 1 tablespoon) olive oil
½ teaspoon salt

Put the flour into a large bowl, make a well in the centre and add the eggs, oil and salt, stirring in gradually. Knead the dough until smooth, then rest for 15 minutes. Roll out the dough into several very thin sheets, sprinkling them with flour and keeping covered with a cloth those you are not working with.

Butter Sauce • see page 68

2 cups fish stock
125 g (4 oz) butter
150 g (5 oz) salted butter, cut into small cubes and frozen
scant 3 (Aus: 2) tablespoons finely chopped chives
a little freshly ground black pepper

Put the fish stock into a saucepan, bring to the boil and cook over high heat until reduced to about 100 ml (3½ fl oz). Add the frozen butter piece by piece, whisking in to form a sauce. Keep in a warm place.

Saffron Custard • see page 74

500 ml (16 fl oz) cream (35% fat content)
1 teaspoon saffron threads
2 large or 3 small whole eggs
3 additional egg yolks
salt and white pepper to taste
dash of Tabasco sauce

Make the custard by heating the cream and saffron until almost boiling. Remove from the heat and leave to infuse for 1 hour, stirring from time to time to prevent a skin from forming on top. Lightly whisk the cream with the whole eggs and egg yolks and season with salt, pepper and Tabasco. Do not whisk the mixture too much and create a foam.

Bush Tomato Salsa • see page 76

¼ cup olive oil
1 medium-sized onion, diced
2½ (Aus: 2) tablespoons curry powder
1 teaspoon chilli powder
salt and pepper to taste
500 g (1 lb) bush tomatoes or sun-dried tomatoes, soaked to soften
500 g (1 lb) sugar
1 cup red wine vinegar
salt and pepper to taste

Heat the oil and sauté the onion, curry powder and chilli powder until the onion softens. Add the tomatoes, sugar and vinegar and simmer uncovered until the tomatoes break up and the sauce thickens. Season to taste with salt and pepper.

Prawn Mousse • *see page 80*

400 g (13 oz) peeled raw prawns
2 egg whites
3 teaspoons lemon juice
pinch sea salt
pinch of freshly ground white pepper
175 ml (scant 6 fl oz) thickened cream

Chop the prawn meat into small chunks. Put this into a food processor with the egg whites, lemon juice, salt and pepper. Process until the mixture becomes a fine paste, then add the cream and blend only just until the mixture adheres; too much processing will cause the mousse to split and fall apart during cooking. The prawn mousse should be quite firm in texture.

Prawn Sauce • *see page 80*

350 g (11 oz) fresh prawn heads
50 ml (1½ fl oz) Chinese *shaoxing* wine
50 ml (1½ fl oz) vegetable oil
1 onion, finely chopped
3 cloves garlic, finely chopped
1 heaped (Aus: 1 level) tablespoon finely
    chopped ginger
1 red or green bird's-eye chilli,
    finely chopped
2 kaffir lime leaves, very finely chopped
1 stalk lemon grass, very finely chopped
1 whole star anise
1 teaspoon coriander seeds
1 teaspoon Sichuan peppercorns
½ teaspoon fennel seeds
5 ripe tomatoes, roasted in a pan in a hot oven
    for 20–25 minutes until slightly blackened
    and soft
3 cups fish stock
250 ml (8 fl oz) thickened cream

fish sauce to taste
lime juice to taste

Sear prawn heads in a hot wok until they begin to turn pink. Add the *shaoxing* wine, stir to deglaze the pan and remove from heat. Heat oil in a saucepan and sauté the onion, garlic, ginger, chilli, lime leaves and lemon grass until the onion turns transparent. Add the spices and stir fry for a couple of minutes. Add the prawn heads and their juices, the roasted tomatoes and any juice from the roasting pan. Put in the fish stock and stir to combine all ingredients.

Bring to the boil, then reduce to a medium simmer and cook for 2 hours, skimming the surface regularly. Pour the stock through a fine mesh sieve, discard the solids and put the strained stock into a clean pan. Bring back to the boil and add the cream. Let it return to the boil and stir to incorporate the cream. Simmer for 15 minutes to allow the sauce to thicken, then add fish sauce and lime juice, a drop at a time, tasting until the sauce is seasoned to your taste. Keep aside, reheating just before serving.

Bush Tomato Chutney • *see page 82*

200 g (7 oz) treacle or golden syrup
100 g (3½ oz) shallots, finely chopped
2½ (Aus: 2) tablespoons finely chopped garlic
2½ (Aus: 2) tablespoons finely chopped ginger
5 medium-sized ripe tomatoes, peeled and
    seeds discarded
1 cup malt vinegar
100 ml (3½ fl oz) vegetable oil
2½ (Aus: 2) tablespoons black mustard seeds
1 cinnamon stick
4 teaspoons salt
200 g (7 oz) dried bush tomatoes or sundried
    tomatoes, soaked to soften

1 red and 1 green bird's-eye chilli, deseeded
and finely chopped
1 whole bunch of coriander, leaves and roots
washed and chopped

Heat the treacle or golden syrup gently in a pan,
then add the shallots, garlic, ginger and tomatoes
and cook for 30 seconds. Add the vinegar and stir
to mix well. Heat the oil in a separate small
saucepan, add the mustard seeds and cover the pan.
When the mustard seeds finish popping, transfer
them to the syrup mix and add all other ingredients.
Simmer the chutney for 15 minutes, then transfer
to a clean jar. Cool and cover.

Lemon Butter Sauce • *see page 82*

125 g (4 oz) butter
50 g (1$\frac{1}{2}$ oz) shallots, finely chopped
1 teaspoon crushed white peppercorns
3 (Aus: 2$\frac{1}{4}$) tablespoons lemon juice
4 teaspoons (Aus: 1 tablespoon) white wine
vinegar
$\frac{1}{2}$ cup dry white wine
1 cup strong fish stock
4 teaspoons (Aus: 1 tablespoon) single cream
salt to taste

Heat the butter in a saucepan, sauté the shallots and
peppercorns until the shallots turn transparent, then
add the lemon juice and vinegar. Stir and reduce
until the mixture is almost dry, then add the white
wine. Add fish stock and simmer uncovered until
reduced by half. Sieve the sauce, put back into a
clean pan, then add the cream and remaining butter, stirring over low heat for 15 minutes. Season
with salt and pepper. Do not bring the sauce back
to the boil as it will separate.

Shepherd's Pie Casing • *see page 106*

300–400 g (10–13 oz) dry mashed potato
1 teaspoon olive oil
1 egg, lightly beaten
salt and pepper to taste

Beat the mashed potato with a wooden spoon until
perfectly smooth. Add oil, egg and seasoning and
beat until well incorporated and smooth.

Shepherd's Pie Filling • *see page 106*

3 large lamb shanks
2 teaspoons butter
2 teaspoons olive oil
$\frac{1}{2}$ stalk celery, chopped
$\frac{1}{2}$ onion, chopped
$\frac{1}{2}$ carrot, chopped
2 cloves garlic
1 bay leaf
1 sprig thyme
2–3 cups lamb stock
1 cup dry white wine

Heat the butter and oil in a heavy saucepan or casse-
role of sufficient size to just hold the lamb shanks.
Brown the shanks on all sides, add the vegetables,
herbs, stock and wine to just cover the shanks. Bring
to the boil, cover, and simmer gently for 1–1$\frac{1}{2}$ hours,
until the meat is sufficiently tender to come off the
bone. Remove the meat. Strain and cool the stock
and adjust seasoning. Cut the meat into chunks, put
back in the stock and refrigerate until required.

Polenta • *see page 108*

8 cups (2 litres) water
4 teaspoons (Aus: 1 tablespoon) olive oil
50 g (1½ oz) butter
375 g (12 oz) polenta
salt to taste
150 g (5 oz) fontina or gruyère cheese, grated

Bring the water to the boil with the oil and butter. When it is bubbling, slowly pour in the polenta, stirring constantly so that no lumps form. When the mixture comes back to the boil, lower the heat, add the salt and cook, stirring constantly, for 45 minutes. If you do not stir the mixture, it will stick to the bottom of the pan. When the polenta is cooked, add the cheese and stir until thoroughly melted. Check the seasoning and pour out into a rectangular container to a depth of about 2 cm (¾ in). Cool for at least 1 hour before cutting into 10 cm (4 in) squares. The polenta will keep up to 5 days refrigerated.

Chick Pea Curry • *see page 110*

400 g (13 oz) chick peas (garbanzos), soaked overnight
scant 3 (Aus: 2) tablespoons vegetable oil
2 onions, coarsely chopped
6 cloves garlic, finely chopped
2.5 cm (1 in) ginger, finely chopped
1 teaspoon turmeric powder
4 teaspoons (Aus: 1 tablespoon) cumin seeds, toasted and ground
1 tin (400 ml/13 fl oz) coconut milk
fresh coriander leaves to garnish

Soak the chick peas in cold water overnight. The following day, drain, simmer in fresh water until almost tender and drain again. Heat the oil and sauté the onion, garlic and ginger until transparent and fragrant, then sprinkle in the turmeric and cumin and sauté for a few seconds. Stir in the coconut milk, then add the chick peas and simmer for about 15 minutes, until the chick peas are soft. The curry can be kept aside and reheated gently immediately before serving.

Harissa • *see page 110*

4–6 cloves garlic
4 teaspoons (Aus: 1 tablespoon) dried mint
4 teaspoons (Aus: 1 tablespoon) chopped fresh mint
4 teaspoons (Aus: 1 tablespoon) freshly ground coriander seeds or coriander powder
4 (Aus: 3) tablespoons fresh coriander leaves
4 teaspoons (Aus: 1 tablespoon) salt
2 teaspoons freshly ground carraway seeds
2 or more chillies (deseeded if you don't want recipe to be too hot)
150 ml (5 fl oz) olive oil

Combine all ingredients and blend or process until you have a thick paste. Store in a covered jar.

Appendix: Contributors

Stephanie Alexander has won numerous personal awards and accolades for Stephanie's, owned by her and partner Dur-é Dara. Listed as Australia's top restaurant and one of the ten best in the world in *Courvoisier's Book of the Best*, Stephanie's opened in Melbourne in 1976. Ms Alexander has led the way in encouraging Australian suppliers to produce world-class raw items, and has written four books for food lovers, including *Stephanie's Australia*.

Guido van Baelen trained in his native Belgium, then worked in Algeria, South Africa and London. In 1988 he was appointed Executive Sous Chef at Cairns Hilton, and for the past 6 years he has been Executive Chef at the Sydney Airport Hilton. He is well known for his creative cooking classes and is an active member of La Chaine des Rotisseurs.

Tony Baker is an Adelaide-based writer, journalist and author, who was born in England and went to Australia in the late 1960s because he had heard the wine was good and cheap. As well as being a daily newspaper editor and columnist, he has written about the Australian good life for almost 20 years for numerous publications.

Maggie Beer, regarded by many as the pioneer of Australian regional cuisines and as "one of the great country cooks of all time", runs the famous Pheasant Farm restaurant at the game farm owned by herself and husband Colin in the Barossa Valley of South Australia.

Beh Kim Un, originally from Penang in Malaysia, grew up surrounded by good food. Shortly after graduating in Industrial Chemistry in Melbourne in 1977, he moved out of the laboratory into the kitchen. His imaginative interpretation of Asian cuisine is given exposure in three Melbourne restaurants, Monsoon, The Isthmus of Kra and Shakahari. He frequently demonstrates in leading cooking schools.

Andrew Blake began working in Melbourne in 1980 at the most famous restaurant of the day, Fanny's, then worked in top Sydney restaurants from 1985 to 1989. Returning to Melbourne, he introduced his signature style to Cafe Kanis, then went on to open Blake's in 1992. He describes his food as "fresh and modern" and is known for his eclectic style.

Marieke Brugman was born in Melbourne to Dutch parents. She left Australia for Europe in 1969, returning to Australia to study Fine Arts. In 1977 she established the Howqua Dale Gourmet Retreat with Sarah Stegley. She later opened the Howqua Dale Cooking School, Australia's only residential participatory programme. She has been in the forefront of the movement to establish fine dining in Australia's rural areas.

Rita Erlich is a senior journalist with the Melbourne newspaper, *The Age*, with a special interest in food and wine. She is the author of a number of books on food and cooking, and the co-editor of the best selling and highly respected annual guide to Victoria's restaurants, *The Age Good Food Guide*.

Cheong Liew grew up in multiracial Malaysia. He came to study in Australia in 1970 and later worked in a variety of European and Asian restaurants in both Melbourne and Adelaide. He became chef at Adelaide Hilton's Grange Restaurant in 1995. Often credited as the first chef in Australia to fully exploit a fusion of several Asian and Western styles, Cheong Liew believes this approach to cooking is only natural in multi–cultural Australia.

Gerda Eilts began her training in her native Germany, then worked in London and South Africa before joining the Hilton International Australia in 1985. She became Executive Sous Chef at Brisbane Hilton in 1990, and Executive Chef at Parmelia Perth Hilton in 1995. One of the new breed of chefs creating a contemporary Australian cuisine, Gerda is also among the few to have earned a degree as a Master Chef.

Andrew Fielke was trained as a cook in his native Adelaide before working in Europe for a few years. Upon returning to Australia, he learned of the budding movement to gather and use wild native ingredients, and started the Red Ochre Grill in 1992 to develop and feature indigenous Australian food. A branch of this restaurant opened in Cairns in 1994. Fielke is also involved in the gathering, growing and production of native foods.

Bethany Finn, Executive Chef of the Adelaide Hilton, began her career in South Australia and then headed for Europe, where she worked in a boutique hotel in Sussex, England. She returned to Adelaide ("the food and wine mecca of Australia"), where she heads a team of 36 chefs. Her style is influenced by the region's Mediterranean climate, Asian ingredients and the finest local produce.

Herbet Franceschini recently celebrated his 30th year with the Hilton International. German-born, he worked in the Americas before com-

ing to Australia to open the Sydney Hilton as Executive Chef in 1974. As Executive Chef of the Brisbane Hilton since 1986, he launched an on-going Guest Chef programme, bringing in top Australian and international chefs, and was host chef at Queensland's inaugural Masterclass Weekend in 1995.

Werner Kimmeringer first donned a cook's apron in his native Bavaria at the age of 14. Since then, he worked in restaurant kitchens around the world, returning to Europe in 1983 and joining the Hilton in Brussels. His innovative work in Sydney Hilton's San Francisco Grill won him awards, and since coming to the Melbourne Hilton in 1991, he has won further accolades as Chef of the Year in Victoria. He has travelled Australia extensively, collecting new ideas and ingredients.

Allan Koh, Executive Chef of Melbourne's trend-setting East-West restaurant, Chinois, began his training in a Japanese restaurant in Kuala Lumpur, Malaysia, at the age of 15, moving on to a Vietnamese restaurant before coming to Australia in 1987. He joined Chinois in 1989, where he creates a distinctive style of food blending Asian and Western ingredients and cooking techniques.

Kurt Looser, Executive Chef of Sydney Hilton, began his career in Switzerland, honing his skills in Lon-

don, Bermuda and the Bahamas before joining the Sydney Hilton in 1973. He moved to Parmelia Perth Hilton in 1979, then returned to Switzerland for 12 months. He was invited back to the Sydney Hilton as Executive Chef in 1981. His style of cuisine is "Australian and international", using imagination and well practised methods of preparation with the best of local produce.

Ashley Mackevicius is one of Australia's leading food photographers whose images of food have graced numerous cookbooks and magazines both in Australia and overseas. He is also the food photographer for this book. His love of food and cooking brings with it a style that is distinctive, modern and very much in tune with contemporary Australian cuisine. He looks forward to showing the rest of the world that Australian food is distinctive and has a quality which ranks it among the world's best.

Tess Mallos, born in Australia of Greek parents, began her career as a consultant in the food industry. She has worked as a cookbook author and food writer for 35 years, as well as being involved in consumer education, advertising and TV cookery programmes. The best known of her many cookbooks are *The Greek Cookbook*, *The Complete Middle East Cookbook*, *The Filo Pastry Cookbook* and *Mediterranean Cooking*.

Christine Manfield, co-owner and chef of the highly acclaimed Paramount Restaurant in Sydney, worked with Philip Searle at Oasis Seros in Sydney and at the Petaluma Restaurant in Adelaide before venturing into business with partner Margie Harris. Her food is intrinsically Australian in technique, style and presentation, with its original blend of assertive flavours and harmonious textures.

Bill Marchetti began training as a chef in his native Italy at the age of 13. He came to Australia in 1968 and in 1984 took over the Latin Restaurant in a famous Melbourne location which has housed an Italian restaurant for more than a century. He regards himself as "a northern Italian traditionalist" in style, and calls Australia "Italy's 22nd region".

Paul Merrony, who was born in Tasmania, trained in the famous Berowra Waters Inn before working as a chef in London and Paris. Since returning to Australia in 1987, he has attracted an enthusiastic following and has won a number of awards. At his Sydney restaurant, Merrony's, he prepares what he terms "new French cooking in Australia".

Damien Pignolet, a second-generation Australian of French origin, trained in Melbourne, where he ran a cooking school and wrote articles for a culinary magazine. He moved to Sydney in 1978 as Executive Chef of Pavilion on the Park. After working in a number of other top restaurants, he and his partner established Bistro Moncur, where Pignolet produces "an Australian interpretation of French cuisine" and continues teaching through his appearances as a guest chef in other Australian cities.

Dietmar Sawyere comes from a family of Swiss restaurateurs, and began working for the Savoy in London at the age of 16. He has worked in some of the world's most exclusive hotels and restaurants since, and won a number of awards. Appointed Executive Chef of the Regent in Melbourne in 1988, he came to Sydney 4 years later and set up Forty One Restaurant, where he concentrates on "bringing back reality to food".

Charmaine Solomon is best known as the woman who brought Asian cooking into Western kitchens with her cookbooks, particularly *The Complete Asian Cookbook*. Born in Sri Lanka, her Dutch Burgher family were renowned for their cooking skills, as was her mother's family in Burma and India. She has lived in Australia for 35 years, sharing her knowledge through the printed medium and TV.

Michael Symons, author of *One Continuous Picnic: A History of Eating in Australia* and *The Shared Table: Ideas for Australian Cuisine*, is completing further titles on the subject of food. He instigated the Symposiums of Australian Gastronomy in Adelaide in 1984 and, inquiring into the peculiar absence of gastronomy from the Academy, completed a Ph.D. in the sociology of cuisine at Flinders University of South Australia in 1991.

Alla Wolf-Tasker, born in Austria of Russian parents, arrived in Australia as a baby and determined at an early age to pursue a career as a chef. After working in restaurants in Australia and Europe, she established a successful cookery school in Melbourne, and opened the Lake House in the scenic Victorian countryside in 1983. She sees her cuisine as being firmly regionally and seasonally based, with emphasis placed on small local rural suppliers, yet also having a certain city sophistication and drawing on traditions from many parts of the world.

Tetsuya Wakuda, who was born in Tokyo, worked in hotels and restaurants there before coming to Australia in 1982. He immediately obtained a position in one of Sydney's top restaurants. In 1986, he opened a restaurant known as Ultimo's and then began what is now regarded as one of Australia's top restaurants, Tetsuya's, in 1989. Tetsuya creates dishes that enhance rather than alter the flavour of the main ingredients, blending Western cooking methods and ingredients with Japanese sensibilities and flavourings.

Index